D1860208

TAMIL WISDOM

Traditions Concerning Hindu Sages
AND
SELECTIONS FROM THEIR WRITINGS

TIRU VALLUVAR.

TAMIL WISDOM

Traditions Concerning Hindu Sages
AND
SELECTIONS FROM THEIR WRITINGS

EDWARD JEWITT ROBINSON

WITH AN INTRODUCTION BY
REV. ELIJAH HOOLE, D. D.

© Author

All rights reserved. No part of this work may be reproduced, stored, adapted, or transmitted in any form or by any means, electronic, mechanical, photocopying, micro-filming, recording or otherwise, or translated in any language, without the prior written permission of the copyright owner and the publisher. The book is sold subject to the condition that it shall not, by way of trade or otherwise, be lent, resold, hired out, or otherwise circulated without the prior publisher's written consent in any form of binding or cover other than that in which it is published.

The views and opinions expressed in this book are author(s) own and the facts reported by them have been verified to the extent possible, and the publishers are not in any way liable for the same.

ISBN : 978-93-5324-515-3 (HB)

First Published, London, 1873

Published, 2020

Published by

Facsimile Publisher
12 Pragati Market
Ashok Vihar, Ph-2
Delhi-110052
E-mail: books@facsimilepublisher.com

Printed at: G. Print Process, Delhi.

Tamil Wisdom

Author: Edward Jewitt Robinson

TAMIL WISDOM;

Traditions Concerning Hindu Sages,

AND

SELECTIONS FROM THEIR WRITINGS.

BY

EDWARD JEWITT ROBINSON.

WITH AN INTRODUCTION BY THE LATE

REV. ELIJAH HOOLE, D.D.

"As certain also of your own poets have said."—Acts xvii. 28.
"One of themselves, even a prophet of their own, said."—Titus i. 12.

LONDON:
WESLEYAN CONFERENCE OFFICE,
2, CASTLE-STREET, CITY-ROAD;
SOLD AT 66, PATERNOSTER-ROW.

1873.

CONTENTS.

INTRODUCTION.

THIS little volume of Heathen morals and learning affords an additional illustration of the truth of the Apostle's words that "the world by wisdom knew not God." Some of the sayings which are here rendered into English are probably as old as the earliest writings of the Old Testament. We have no evidence that the art of writing was practised before the Deluge; but it is demonstrated that in many lands it was commenced very soon after that event. The earliest records we have are those of Egypt. These were known to Moses, who was "learned in all the wisdom of the Egyptians." In the Egyptian records, alphabetical letters were mixed with hieroglyphical signs. The Phenicians appear to have selected a few of these letters for mercantile purposes, from which all the alphabets of Europe in due time were formed. The written characters of India, those of Tamil among the number, appear to have been derived from Deva-Nagiri, which probably had the same origin. In those early days, it is evident, there was communication from one part of the world to another more free than in later times. The system of alphabetical writing did not occur to the Chinese. They use signs, not letters. But the relationship of those remote people to the western nations is now receiving new proof from the labours of the Rev. J. Edkins, who is publishing a series of papers on the "Connection of Chinese and Hebrew." Encouraged by the success of the process adopted by Mr. Edkins, another gentleman versed in the Chinese has begun a series of papers, under the signature of Ossian, proving the connection between the Gaelic and the Chinese!

Words and idioms occur in Tamil which remind the student of parallels in Hebrew.

There are very few historical records in the Tamil language. Fables and moral sayings in verse, having a strong hold on the memory, have been preserved through the revolutions of four thousand years, while history has perished. Perhaps if we had the songs and sayings of our ancestors of four thousand years ago, they would be equally interesting.

The acquisition of the language in which the remains of Tamil wisdom are preserved, is no easy task. Aptitude, genius, industry, perseverance, are necessary to the Tamil scholar. . . . Next to taking the Gospel to the Heathen, . . . he who brings them, in their manners and minds, to the knowledge of the followers of Christ, confers on them a benefit which it is not easy to estimate.

The reader will acknowledge that God "left not

Himself without witness" among the Tamil people. "There is a spirit in man: and the inspiration of the Almighty giveth them understanding." The maxims and morals of the ancients, preserved in the traditions of the people, prevented society from falling into entire barbarism, and in principle, at the least, anticipated the Christian rule which now prevails to the great advantage of all classes of the natives of India.

ELIJAH HOOLE.

8, MYDDELTON SQUARE,
30*th March*, 1872.

Note.—The foregoing interesting and instructive Introduction was kindly written by the late senior Secretary of the Wesleyan-Methodist Missionary Society, at the considerate suggestion of the Rev. Dr. Jobson, to whom, therefore, as well as on other grounds, thanks are sincerely tendered. It is the more valuable as possibly the latest production of the able pen of the accomplished and honoured minister, the news of whose death sent a pang to many hearts, not in England only, but in the country in which he was formerly a laborious and successful missionary. Since he left India, his friendly and judicious letters have edified and comforted numbers of his successors in that great field of missionary enterprise; and his excellent versions in Tamil of some of Wesley's hymns continue to be sung there in the Christian places of worship. It is known to have been a wish of his that the *Cural* should be translated into English metre.

TAMIL WISDOM;

TRADITIONS CONCERNING HINDU SAGES, AND SELECTIONS FROM THEIR WRITINGS.

Language and Literature.

TAMIL is to be respected as having been the adopted tongue of Beschi, Ziegenbalg, Schwartz, and Fabricius. It was the first of the languages of India studied by Protestant Missionaries, and is that with which the Jesuit propagandists have been mostly exercised. It has attracted the attention of many learned civilians; and Europeans have probably spoken and written more in it, especially in the common or lower dialect, than in any other eastern language.

The oldest treatise on Tamil was composed by a sage called Agastya, who is therefore regarded as its founder, and is honoured as a god. As its name imports, it is truly a *sweet* tongue. The Tamils call Sanscrit "*Vada-morlyi*," *the northern speech*, supposing it to have originated in the north, and their own language "*Ten-morlyi*," *the southern speech*, because

Pothiyamalay, the mountain in which Agastya lived, is in the south of India. A sufficient reason for the name is, that in fact Tamil is the southern language, being used by ten millions of people, in that part of Hindustan formerly comprising the Chēra, Chōla, and Pandiya kingdoms, and in the northern half of the island of Ceylon.

Cities conversed in it centuries before the Christian era; and, as might be inferred from its beauty and finish, it boasts an ancient and honoured literature. In a valuable publication from the Jaffna press,* a native gentleman records the names of one hundred and ninety-six Tamil authors. The history of not a few of them is inextricably blended with fable, and many of their compositions are irrecoverably lost; but they have bequeathed writings of a character inviting close examination, and sufficiently copious to demand persevering research.

There are two orders of Tamil classics; *Ilakkanam*, philology and the art of composition, and *Ilakkiyam*, correctly executed works, mythological, epic, and didactic. The most respected of the moral poems are those which, like the *Cural*, obtained the approval of the celebrated Madura College.

"The inducements held out to poets, and the rewards bestowed on them by the long line of Pandiya kings, who graced the throne of Madura from the ninth century before to the fourteenth century

* The Tamil Plutarch. By Simon Casie Chitty, Esq.

after Christ, were most liberal, and might have done honour even to the court of Augustus. These kings had three different *Sangams*, or colleges, established in their capital at three different periods, for the promotion of literature, more or less corresponding in character with the Royal Academy of Sciences founded by Louis XIV. at Paris; and made it a rule that every literary production should be submitted to their *Senatus Academicus* before it was allowed to circulate in the country, for the purpose of preserving the purity and integrity of the language. It may be well imagined how favourably these *Sangams* operated on the talent and genius of the nation. From every part of Southern India poets crowded into the *Sanga-mandapam*, or College-hall, to recite their compositions; and the successful candidate, besides winning the smiles of Royalty, was rewarded with something more enduring and substantial. Neither were the kings of Chēra and Chōla backward in patronizing poets, for they had a certain number of them always attached to their courts. There can be no doubt that an infinite number of works in the different departments of science and literature was composed during this brilliant age; but in the early part of the fourteenth century, when the Mohammedan hordes poured into Southern India, and Prākrama-Pandiyan was led away captive to Delhi, the Tamils had to deplore the loss of almost all their literature; for those ruthless fanatics, amongst other outrages, ransacked all the libraries in the country, and committed to the flames 'all that genius had reared for ages.'"*

Some of the papers following have already seen the light; but the work that contained them had scarcely begun to circulate, when the copies in stock perished in a fire. The translations of the *Cural* and *Mariyāthay-Rāman* in this volume are now published for the first time. The concluding paper is a rendering of a prose composition in the spoken language. The versions of the *Cural*, *Muthuray*, and *Agaval* are from writings in the poetic dialect and form, in which all the most ancient Tamil books extant, on whatever subject, are composed.

Few as are these samples of eastern wit and story, the writer deems it his duty to give them to the public. He would have them regarded as a hint of much work of the sort remaining to be done by missionaries and other Christian residents in the Tamil country. They are particularly commended to the notice of the friends of Missions, as indicating a peculiar feature in the character of the Hindus, their superiority in civilization and culture to the heathens of other lands, and the delicacy and difficulty of the work of the missionary in India. Let the evangelist only call them to a virtuous life, and they will reply that their own moral maxims are as good as his, and, the conduct of some Europeans on their shores and in their towns considered, not less effective. They

* Tamil Plutarch.

need more than to be pointed to the remaining flowers of the ancient paradise, and charmed by Vedantic teaching like Rammohun-Roy's and Chunder-Sen's. It is necessary to tell them of the Lamb, by Whom only they can obtain forgiveness of sins, and power to keep God's eternal law. The young missionary does much who simply describes and recommends the Gospel. To cry aloud, with praying zeal, "God so loved the world, that He gave His only-begotten Son, that whosoever believeth in Him should not perish, but have everlasting life," is to awake attention, touch the heart, and win souls to Christ. The evident sincerity of the preacher commands respect for both himself and his message; and for a certain class of estimable ministers it is better that they should continue only to proclaim the naked truth in Jesus, and not fetter themselves by affecting a knowledge of Hindu literature and opinion. But it would be a calamity if there were no experienced missionaries intimately acquainted with the admirable writings of which the people are justly proud, and respecting which the remark may be sometimes encountered, that they are comparable with the Book of Proverbs and the Sermon on the Mount.

As the wise sayings of India come before the British public, they must have the advantage of appearing alone. The company in which some of them are found could scarcely be introduced into the English language. This is an important fact, not to be overlooked in missionary considerations. If moral maxims could themselves do good, their useful power is lost in evil associations. Not only side by side with those of India, but interwoven with the language of many of them, are statements and doctrines most immoral. The ethical rules of the Tamils are hung, darkened with foul devices, about the cars and temples of idolatry, and spoken from pagan altars which convey no moral inspiration. The missionary has to separate them from the rubbish which buries them, and attach them to their home, the atoning and cleansing Cross. He has to train his converts to combat the errors of Hinduism, while respecting whatever truths are in it, as the Christians of the early centuries, upholding the universal moral law, found it necessary to sweep away the mythological abominations of the Greeks and Latins by which it was trammelled and obscured. Always foolishness without the light of Christ, the wisdom of this world is most foolish in the writings and sayings of actual pagans.

The Outcast Children.

IN the subjoined history, compiled from accounts that differ in some particulars, the reader is left to distinguish the probable from the incredible. Veracious Hindu biographers are unknown.

About the ninth century of the Christian era, somewhere in the fertile Chōla country, a Brahman's house was filled with rejoicing on occasion of the birth of a boy. His delighted father named him Pagavan. There is bitterness in the sweetest cup. The blossoms of happiness are too often blighted. In a few days, the good man appeared before his wife with a sorrowful face, announcing as a revelation of the horoscope that their child would some day marry a low-caste girl. What could be done to avert, if possible, a calamity so dire? He would go on pilgrimage to the Ganges. Thither he went.

It may be lamented that he flourished in a degenerate day. In former times, the husband's excellence was imputed to the wife, and a Brahman might have ventured to predict a bright career and illustrious posterity for his son. Menu wrote:—"Whatever be the qualities of the man with whom a woman is united by lawful marriage, such qualities even she assumes, like a river united with the sea. Acshamala, a woman of the lowest birth, being thus united to Vasishtha, and Sarangi being united to Mandapala, were entitled to very high honour. These, and other females of low birth, have attained eminence in this world by the respective good qualities of their lords." Had the father of Pagavan not lived in the iron age, there would have been no necessity to feel so distressed at the prospect which the horoscope unfolded.

The pensive woman, waiting many years without welcoming her husband's return, found her highest pleasure in watching over her beautiful boy, and securing to him the best education. Clever and studious, the youth well repaid her kindness. When fifteen years old, he was revered by all as learned in the Vēda. At this period he obtained from his mother an answer to a question with which he had often troubled her, "Why did my father leave you?" Greatly grieved to discover the reason, he determined to follow his pious parent, and at once set out as a pilgrim to Casi (Benares).

When, in a rest-house on the way, Pagavan had concluded his daily devotions, and was preparing himself some food, a simple girl appeared in his presence. "What low-caste thing are you, presuming to come here?" exclaimed the resolute and circumspect young gentleman; and in his anger he threw, some say the wooden spoon with which he was cooking, others a stone, at the innocent damsel. Wounded on the head, she ran crying to Mēlūr, the adjoining village, in which dwelt her Brahman foster-father, Nithiyayan. The choleric pilgrim, having quickly bathed and eaten, resumed his journey.

On his return from his vain search for his father, Pagavan ventured to stop at the same choultry as before. The maiden again made her appearance. He did not recognize her; and she was now beautiful as Lakshmi, and under the powerful protection of the god of love. Nithiyayan, who owned the rest-house, perceiving that the traveller's affections were captivated, and wishing to do the best he could for his adopted daughter, said to him, "Marry my child, and abide with us." He replied,—"I will do so when"—pointing to a jar of water which he had brought on his shoulder from the Ganges—"I have presented this offering at Ramesuram (Ramisseram)."

As soon as possible, the young Brahman was back again, where he had left his heart and treasure, at Mēlūr. Nithiyayan's relatives were assembled for the marriage. On the fifth day of the feast, the time having come for the bridegroom to pour oil on the head of his bride, arranging her soft hair for the purpose, he discovered a scar. Memory was awake in a moment, suggesting terrible fears and doubts. He asked, "Are you not Athy-al?" that is, "the girl

I first met with?" Not waiting for an answer, he ran away. By her reputed father's advice, Athy, known ever after by the name her husband thus gave her, followed. It was a toilsome pursuit; but she found him at length resting in a shed in a low-caste village. She said to him pitifully, "God having united us, is it kind or right to forsake me in this way? I cannot live in your absence." After a minute's consideration, he replied,—"Woman, if you love me, agree to what I propose. You may accompany me on one condition, that, whenever a child is born, you abandon it then and there." She reluctantly consented.

Three sons and four daughters appeared in succession, in the rest-house, in the grove, or on the mountain-side, as they travelled. On the birth of each, Athy, with her foot rooted to the ground, exclaimed in agony, "O, who will take care of my babe?" In every instance, the infant gave a wise and encouraging answer; upon hearing which, the mother went resolutely on her way. The consoling sayings of the marvellous children are known as "The Song of the Seven."

SONG OF THE SEVEN.

UPPAY.

Shall Nari's lord * the rain command,
And dew, to feed the thorny trees
Which in the tangled forest stand,
Where eye of mortal never sees,
And not my daily food supply,
But leave his votary to die?

OUVVAY.

Why, mother, snatch me from the ground?
Of living things am I not one?
Preserving life wherever found,
Is there a God, or is there none?
To fate with faith surrender me:
Whatever is to be will be.

URUVAY.

The lively chick that breaks the shell
May guardian grace and power attest,
And nourish'd infancy dispel
The doubts that tear thy troubled breast:
In Aran's † name of truth and power,
Find firmness for the evil hour.

* Parvati's husband: Siva. † Siva.

VALLY.

Whose head the serpent's gleams adorn,
Who dances at the Vēda's end,
Who cherish'd me when yet unborn,
Will Peruman* not still befriend?
The future's written in the past:
His providence must ever last.

ATHIGAMAN.

Be strong in heart: is Siva dead?
According to his gracious will,
He wrote my doom within my head;
And will he not my fate fulfil?
If famine come, not thine the care;
The burden is for him to bear.

VALLUVAR.

On whom ovarian life depends,
The rock-encompass'd frog who feeds,
The True One pitifully sends
Whate'er thy helpless offspring needs:
O, make his sovereign care thy choice,
And weep not, mother, but rejoice.

* Siva.

CABILAR.

My all since I began to be,
  How shall he now refuse to keep?
Can he evade himself or me?
  Or can his eye be seal'd in sleep?
Or can dismay his mind confound,
Like thine in love and trouble drown'd?

Taking them in the above order, the sayings are sometimes attributed consecutively to Cabilar, Valluvar, Uruvay, Vally, Ouvvay, Athigaman, and Uppay.

The Life of Valluvar.

IT is not known when this illustrious Tamil flourished. Some say as early as the third or fourth century of the Christian era. Others conclude, with more probability, that he lived in the eighth or ninth.

Hindu poets have not been wont to connect their names with their writings; and their commentators have not always been careful to preserve or ascertain them. The name of the great man who composed the *Cural* has hence been lost. He has been called TIRU-VALLUVAR, till that descriptive title has come to be universally used as his real name. "*Tiru*" means *holy*, *reverend*, *divine;* and "*Valluvar*" is the appellation by which a priest or sage of the Pariah tribe is known. That he was a Pariah, no one doubts. It is contended, however, that if his mother belonged to the low class, yet his father was a Brahman. His history, like that of his alleged brothers and sisters, is buried in the adornments of fabulous tradition. He is regarded as having been an incarnation of Siva. We can do no better than take him up where we left him, and repeat what is written and believed concerning THE DIVINE PARIAH.

Our first sight of him is in a grove of Ilupay trees, at Mayilāpūr, near Madras. He lay exposed, a new-born babe, subsisting on the honey that dropped from the flowers of the trees. Contiguous to the grove was a temple sacred to Siva. Thither came the wife of a Velālan of high rank, paying offerings and worship with a view to being blessed with a son. Parvati, the god's consort, took pity on her, and said, "Adopt this divine infant," naming it Tiru-Valluvar. The delighted lady carried the babe home, and gave it into her husband's hands; and he received it with a thrill of pleasure. They carefully nursed it from day to day, till, their relatives saying contemptuously, "They bring up any child, they do not know whose," they became intimidated, and hung up a swinging-cot in a cow-shed adjacent. Therein they laid the infant, appointing a Pariah family to protect and tend it; and it throve very well.

When five years old, seeing how his father and mother, as he condescended to call them, were scorned by their kindred on his account, he looked on them, and said,—"There is no need that I should cause you affliction. I will be off to another place. Do not trouble about me." They answered, "Let it not be so. Can you speak thus? We thought you a great one, come to put an end to our childlessness." The divinity in him replied, "You have only to think of me at any time, and I am with you, to render you any aid." Then he departed, and rested, near the village, in the shadow of a palmyra-tree, a tall thin tree, the least likely to afford any shelter. Observing that the shadow of the tree never left its foot, the people burst into exclamations of astonishment and praise, saying, "This child is either a sage or a god." The divine boy turned to them, and said,—"What worth or glory is there here? There is nothing in me. Get away." He himself left the place, and repaired to the mountain where Tiru-Mūlar, Pōgar, and other sage and learned personages dwelt, and joined them in their penitential rites and other pious duties.

Seeing him, Tiru-Mūlar said, "O Valluvar, in old time, when I was favoured to dwell in Siva's paradise, you were there. Have you become incarnate, and approached us, to bless the inhabitants of the world with prosperity and joy? Are you about to teach them concerning virtue, wealth, and pleasure, in the language which is sweet?" Thus flattered and encouraged, he gladly made himself one of those who pursued their studies and devotions in that place; and soon he was learned in all the scriptures.

A plainer story may be dismissed in a sentence, that a Valluvan, or priest of the Pariah tribe, found the deserted child, and reared him as his own.

Once when a demon was ravaging the country, destroying the crops, and killing men and beasts, a Velālan named Markasagāyan, who lived at Cāveri-pākam, and owned a thousand yoke of cattle, promised great riches, a house and land, and every requisite, to any one who should subdue the monster. None being able to claim the reward, the wealthy farmer went and told the great personages of the mountain. "Consult Tiru-Valluvar," they said. He did so, with worship; and the young sage, spreading ashes on his hand, and writing thereon the five sacred letters, repeating over them *mantras*, and scattering them in the air, destroyed the depredator, and saved the people's property and lives. Seeing his superhuman greatness, the Velālan, in addition to the estate and untold money, offered him in marriage his only daughter Vāsugy. Impressed with the necessity of practically showing to the world the virtues of the domestic life, he engaged,—"She shall be my wife, if she will take from me sand, and return it in the shape of boiled rice." The maiden accepted the challenge, cooked the earth, and produced the food. Valluvar enjoyed the wonderful meal, and was married to her in the usual way; and he remained in the place a few days.

He then went with his wife to his native town, Mayilāpūr, built himself a house, and illustrated the virtues of the married state. Saying, "The business of weaving is without sin," he purchased thread of a merchant named Elēlasingan, and, whatever became of the presents of his father-in-law, lived, like other Pariahs, on the profits of the loom.

He continued to work wonders, of some of which

Elēlasingan was the subject or a witness. One day, when Valluvar called at his house for some thread, the good merchant worshipped him, saying, "Swamy, take me from the sea of desire, and make me ascend the shore." To test his worth, and that of a few other disciples, he led them into the jungle, and there caused to rise before them a spreading flood. They opened their eyes, and stood trembling, except Elēlasingan, who followed him as he walked on; and as the master and his worthy disciple approached, the water shrank away. He afterwards told him to climb to the top of a high tree; and when he had done so, he said, "Lift your feet from the branch you are standing on, and let go the branch you have hold of." Elēlasingan obeyed, and received no hurt. Valluvar therefore took him into confidence, instructed him in wisdom, and endued him with a will proof against the strongest charms. They then returned to their homes.

The occupant of the throne mockingly advised Elēlasingan to apply to his guru for the gift of children. He did so; and Valluvar answered, "Siva will favour you." Going as usual to visit the cow they daily worshipped, the merchant and his wife found Siva himself as a babe lying and crying at the beast's side. The happy woman took and showed it to Valluvar, by whom it was named Arlyakānanthar. Her husband told the king, who unbelievingly replied, "If the child has come to you from the swamy, let it also come to me." It was in a moment in the rajah's lap; and the queen was joyfully nursing it before long.

A ship belonging to Elēlasingan ran aground; and he informed the king. "What can I do?" his majesty said, "tell your priest." Valluvar fastened a rope to the vessel, at which many sailors pulled in vain till they were exhausted. He then touched the ship with his holy hand, and ordered them to try again; and they were immediately successful.

There came a time of drought and dearth, when many people perished because they could buy no corn. Valluvar said to Elēlasingan, "While the famine lasts, sell the paddy you have bought and stored for the price you gave for it; but always give a quantity over." He did so, and for seven years the rice remained undiminished. His wealth grew to a mountain. On rain falling at length, Valluvar said, "Sell at the same price; but now give short measure in the same proportion." He obeyed; and before the next day's sunset, all the store was gone. Then the divine man commanded, "Melt together the money you have got by selling the paddy, and throw it into the sea." So he did; and a great fish swallowed it. A few days after, the fish was caught; and the fishermen found in it what looked like a black old stone. This they gave to Elēlasingan. Believing it to be what it seemed, he put it into the water to stand upon when bathing

The blackness gradually wore away; and at last the mass shone. Discovering his name miraculously cut in it, he exclaimed, "The guru's grace!" and knew it to be the treasure he had thrown away.

Arlyakānanthar, the son given miraculously to Elēlasingan, having become an illustrious personage, waited, with other learned friends, on Tiru-Valluvar, and said, "Write an ethical treatise for the world's good." Collecting the essence of the Vēdas, he accordingly composed, in 1,330 distichs, a work on the three subjects, Virtue, Wealth, and Pleasure. His friends advised, "O divine man, go with it, and triumph over the college of the doctors!" He set out, leaving his wife at home. Approaching Iday-karlyi, he met Ouvvay and Idaykādan, to whom he told the object of his journey. Idaykādan said, "Siva has cursed the college, saying, 'Let it be destroyed by the middle and the lowest.' It may therefore be defeated by me and you. Let us go along with you." Having reached Madura, and walked round the temple, they entered the presence of Siva and his consort. Before the god, and in the hearing of the Pandiyan king, and his ministers, chiefs, and people, as well as Ouvvay, Idaykādan, and other famous persons, he submitted the three divisions of divine couplets he had prepared. The assembly of professors were alarmed; but joy rose in the breasts of others, who heaped praises on the new poet.

Valluvar, Idaykādan, Ouvvay, and others, joined to

humble the courage and self-conceit of the college. Coming before the doctors, who sat as kings of the sweet tongue on the bench of poets by the tank covered with the golden lotus, who had detected hundreds of errors in the compositions of the most skilful, and even dared to say to Siva, on his appearing to favour an author, "Though you show us your frontal eye, a fault is a fault," so incurring his malediction spoken of, and who deemed themselves more learned than Agastya, the Pariah poet Tiru-Valluvar, like a tiger entering a flock of sheep, or a kite pouncing on a group of serpents, or a lion fighting a herd of elephants, or fire devouring a bamboo forest, easily answered in high Tamil, and baffled all their questions.

The learned assembly said, "O Valluvar, there is yet a doubt on our minds as to whether we can receive the *Cural* you have sung. The bench on which we sit will make room for a treatise in pure Tamil. Let that sign be given, and we shall all consent." The scorned Pariah-born poet laid his book thereupon; and the seat immediately contracted itself to the size of it, so that all the professors fell into the lotus pond. The spectators exultingly applauded; and the forty-nine doctors, scrambling out of the water, mortified exceedingly, yet felt constrained each to pronounce a stanza in praise of Valluvar and the holy *Cural.*

These forty-nine impromptu verses, it is said, have

been preserved. There is at any rate a collection of stanzas in honour of Tiru-Valluvar, attributed to the professors of the Madura College, each with its reputed author's name affixed. The following are specimens.

"The moon full of Kalei (the whole of her face being illuminated) pleases the external eyes, in like manner as the *Cural* full of Kalei (knowledge) pleases the intellectual eyes; but nevertheless she cannot be compared to Valluvar's production, for she is neither spotless, nor does she retain her form and splendour unchanged like it."—*Akārakani-Natshumanār.*

"The gods have known the taste of ambrosia by having partaken of it; but men will know it when they imbibe the milk issuing from the three teats (parts) of the *Cural.*"—*Ālangkudi-Vanganār.*

"Who but Valluvar is able to separate, according to their order, all the things blended together in the Vēdas, and impart them to the world in a condensed form and with due amplification?"—*Arisitkirlyār.*

"Valluvar's *Cural* is short in words, but extensive in sense, even as in a drop of water on the blade of the millet might be seen reflected the image of the tall palmyra-tree."—*Cabilar, the poet's brother.*

"Of the six sects, one will condemn the system of the other; but none of them will condemn the system propounded by Valluvar in his *Cural:* it has the merit of harmonizing the opinions of them all, so that each sect would admit it to be its own."—*Calādar.*

"He who studies the two-lined verses in the three divisions of Valluvar's *Cural,* will obtain the four things (virtue, wealth, pleasure, and eternal happiness); for they contain the substance of the five Vēdas (including the Mahābhārat), and the six systems of the six sects."—*Calattūr-Kirlyār.*

"It is no other than Ayan (Brahma) himself, seated on the beautiful lotus-flower, who, assuming the form of Valluvar, has given to the world the truths of the Vēdas, that they may shine without being mixed up with falsehood."—*Cārikananār.*

"The short distichs which the learned poet Valluvar has composed in order that we may know the ancient right way, are sweet to the mind to meditate on; sweet to the ear to hear; and sweet to the mouth to repeat; and they moreover form a sovereign medicine to promote good and prevent evil actions."—*Cavuniyanār.*

"The Brahmans preserve the four Vēdas orally, and never commit them to writing, because if read by all they would be less valued; but the *Cural* of Valluvar, though committed to writing and read by all, would nevertheless not lose its value."—*Cothamanār.*

"As the *Cural* of Valluvar causes the lotus-flower of the heart to expand, and dispels from it the darkness which cannot otherwise be dispelled, it may well be compared to the hot-rayed sun, which causes the lotus-flower of the tank to expand, and dispels the darkness from the face of the earth."—*Culapathiyār.*

"The *Cural* which has proceeded from the mouth of Valluvar, the king of poets, will never lose its beauty by the lapse of time: it will be always in its bloom, shedding honey like the flower of the tree in Indra's paradise."—*Irayanār.*

"What is the use of works of great length, when the short work of Valluvar alone is enough to edify the world? It contains all things, and there is nothing which it does not contain."—*Madura-Tamil-Nayaganār.*

"Valluvar is in reality a god; and if any shall say that he is a mere mortal, not only will the learned reject his saying, but take him for an ignorant man." —*Māmūlanār.*

"The beauty of Valluvar's *Cural* is, that it not only illustrates the abstruse doctrines of the Vēdas, but is itself a Vēda, easy to be studied, and having the effect of melting the hearts of the righteous who study it." —*Māngudi-Maruthanār.*

"All are relieved of their headache by smelling the sindil-salt, and sliced dry ginger mixed with honey; but Sāttanār (a fellow-professor) was relieved of his head-ache (brought on by his habit of striking his head with his stylus when he found a fault in an author) by hearing the three parts of the *Cural* recited."—*Maruttuvan-Tāmōtharanār.*

"It is no wonder if those who have bathed in the water of a tank abounding with lotus-flowers will not desire to bathe in any other water; but it is a wonder indeed if they who have read Valluvar's work will desire to read any other work."—*Nāgan-Dēvanār.*

"They say that Siva is the patron of North Madura, but this poet who pours out instruction in honeyed words with a parental solicitude, is the patron of South Madura abounding with water."—*Nalkūr-Vēlviyār.*

"Valluvar has lighted a lamp for dispelling the darkness from the hearts of those who live in the world; having virtue for its bowl, wealth for its wick, pleasure for its oil, the fire of expression for its flame, and the short stanza for its stand."—*Napālattanār.*

"Māl (Vishnu) in his *Cural* (or dwarfish incarnation) measured the whole earth with his two expanded feet; but Valluvar has measured the thoughts of all mankind with his (stanza of) two short feet."—*Paranar.*

"It is said that the *Cural* (meaning Vishnu in his incarnation as a dwarf) produced by Casypa in times of yore measured the earth; but the *Cural* now produced by Valluvar has measured both the earth and the heaven."—*Ponmudiyār.*

"To call anyone a poet upon this earth besides the divine Valluvar, would be like calling both the evening illumined by the moon, and the evening shrouded in darkness, a fine evening."—*Sengkundūrkirlyār.*

"By the *Cural*, the production of the divine Tiru-Valluvar, the world has been enabled to distinguish truth from falsehood, which were hitherto confounded together."—*Tēnikudikīranār.*

"The great poet's work comprises everything; or, if there be anything which it does not comprise, he alone knows it."—*Todittalay-Virlyuttandinār.*

"The Four-faced (Brahma), disguising himself as Valluvar, has imparted the truths of the four Vēdas in the three parts of the *Cural*, which is therefore to be adored by the head, praised by the mouth, pondered by the mind, and heard by the ears."—*Ukiraperuvarlyuthiyār.*

"They who have not studied the *Cural* of the divine Valluvar are incapable of good actions: neither their tongues have expressed what is sweet in language, nor their minds understood what is sublime in sense."—*Urayūr-Muthukūtanār.*

"Water springs forth when the earth is dug, and milk when the child sucks the mother's breast, but knowledge when the poets study Valluvar's *Cural.*"—*Uruttirasanmar.*

"It is difficult to say whether the Sanskrit or the Tamil is the best: they are perhaps on a par, since the Sanskrit possesses the Vēda, and the Tamil the

Cural, composed by the divine Valluvar."—*Vanakanshattanār.*

Idaykādan, the friend who had accompanied Valluvar to Madura, to be present when he should submit the *Cural* to the college bench, though not himself one of the professors, could not be silent. Having heard the forty-nine, he thus gave his opinion :—"The *Cural* contains much in a little compass. Such is the ingenuity of its author, that he has compressed within its narrow limits all the branches of knowledge, as if he had hollowed a mustard seed, and enclosed all the waters of the seven seas in it." Hearing this comparison, Ouvvay remarked to him that it would have been more appropriate to liken her brother's *Cural* to an atom, which is even smaller than a mustard seed.*

The captivated college, enraptured king, and others, while congratulating Valluvar, suggested, "If Agastya also accept the work, it will be well." The poet accordingly obtained grace to visit Pothiyamalay, where he occasioned vast delight, and was praised in many songs.

The above commendations are borne out in a degree by the opinions of later and more sober critics. "It is difficult," says the accomplished Ceylon patriot, Simon Casie Chitty, "to judge from the tenor of his *Cural* to what sect he belonged: for he has entirely avoided in the work everything that savours of sec-

* Tamil Plutarch.

tarianism, in order to harmonize the suffrages of all the sects. The Jainas, however, claim him to belong to their sect, from his having used in one of his distichs in praise of God the epithet *Andanan*, which is applicable to *Arukan*, the object of their worship."

It may be more satisfactory to inquire in what estimation the *Cural* is held by judicious and learned Europeans. It "is a poetic work on morals, of great merit as a literary performance," says the Rev. Elijah Hoole, D.D. "The author commences his book with an acknowledgment of God, in a style which, in the production of a heathen, we cannot but greatly admire; and throughout the whole he evinces a singular degree of freedom from many of the strong prejudices of the Hindus, although he frequently illustrates his positions by allusions to the mythology and doctrines of the superstition of his country." A distinguished agent of the London Missionary Society, the Rev. W. H. Drew, by whom a portion of the poem has been rendered into English, says:—"The *Cural* has a strong claim upon our attention, as a part of the literature of the country, and as a work of intrinsic excellence. The author, passing over what is peculiar to particular classes of society, and introducing such ideas only as are common to all, has avoided the uninteresting details of observances found in Menu and the other shastras; and thus in general maintains a dignified style; though it must be acknowledged that he sometimes descends to puerilities. The third part could not be read with impunity by the purest mind, nor translated into any European language without exposing the translator of it to infamy." The Rev. Peter Percival, famous for the laborious and beautiful revision of the Tamil Version of the Holy Bible, made by him while a Methodist missionary in Jaffna, now a clergyman of the Episcopal church and professor of oriental languages in Madras, has published extracts from the *Cural* which, he says, "will be read with pleasure, as affording proof of the existence of the loftiest sentiments, the purest moral rules, and equal power of conception and expression. Nothing certainly, in the whole compass of human language, can equal the force and terseness of the sententious distichs in which the author conveys the lessons of wisdom he utters."

The *Cural* consists of 133 chapters, each containing 10 couplets. Omitting those on Pleasure, 108 ask for a metrical English dress. We only versify the first 24 chapters, hoping that, in better style, some brother in India will render the remaining 84.

This poem is the only composition of any magnitude attributed to the divine Pariah. Visiting such places in returning as he had not called at on his way to Madura, he recited it to delighted hundreds. As he approached Mayilāpūr, his fellow-townsmen, with Elēlasingan at their head, met him with joyful excitement, and conducted him in triumph to his dwelling. Warmly welcomed by Vāsugy, he resumed his homely life of exemplary virtue.

In the *Garland of Advice for Women*, translated in the present volume, the young lady is instructed to perform domestic duties as did the wife of Valluvar. It is therefore important to ascertain how tradition depicts her virtues. We have seen how, rather than not do what she was bid, she metamorphosed a handful of earth into a dish of cooked rice. She was as obedient after marriage as before. A notable personage, presenting himself one day at Valluvar's house, said, "Swamy, graciously inform your servant which is better—a married life, or the life of a lonely hermit." Many days he waited vainly for a verbal answer. The philosopher had his own ways of settling questions. During his visitor's sojourn, he called Vāsugy when she was in the act of drawing water from the well: she left the vessel suspended half way, and hastened to her husband. One morning, when she was serving up cold rice boiled the day before, he exclaimed, "This is burning me:" she ran for a fan, and cooled him. On another occasion, at bright noon-day, when Valluvar was engaged in his occupation as a weaver, his shuttle missed, and dropped to the ground, where it could be distinctly seen: he directed his wife to fetch a light, and she brought it. Witnessing occurrences like these, the visitor concluded, "If such a wife can be had, it is wise to marry; if not, the monastic state were better."

Without a syllable having fallen from the lips of the weaver-sage in reply to his question, he went away enlightened.

At length the darkest of shadows fell on Valluvar. Vāsugy, at the point of death, was looking inquiringly into his face. He affectionately demanded, "What?" "I wish to know," said she, "why, on the day you married me, you directed me always to bring a needle to you, and a vessel of water, when serving you with rice?" He replied "In order that, if a sacred grain should fall, I might pick it up with the needle, and wash it in the water." Receiving this information, she contentedly went to heaven. No rice having ever fallen from her careful husband's hand, she knew not till now the reason of a command which she had ever obeyed, but of which it would have been unseemly before to request an explanation. The loss of such a wife was no light bereavement. Lying sleepless and agitated the night after her decease, the poet extemporarily complained :—

"Dost thou depart, who did'st prepare
My savoury food with skilful care;
On whom alone of womankind,
In ceaseless love, I fix'd my mind;
Who from my door hast never stirr'd,
And never hast transgress'd my word;
Whose palms so softly chafed my feet,
Till charm'd I lay in slumbers sweet;

Who tendedst me with wakeful eyes—
The last to sleep, the first to rise?
Now weary night denies repose:
Can sleep again my eyelids close?"

He buried her sacred body in a sitting posture.

Surviving his wife for many years, and continuing to perform many glorious deeds, Valluvar favoured and helped to the utmost Elēlasingan and his other disciples. At last he summoned his friend to him, and graciously directed him thus:—"The region of completeness is near me. When I am perfected, tie my body with cords, and draw it outside the town, and throw and leave it among the bushes." Seeing him to be like one whose penance and meditations were consummated, Elēlasingan was preparing to place him in a golden coffin, and deposit him in a worthy grave. Whereupon Valluvar awoke, looked at him, graciously remonstrated, "Dear man, do not transgress my word;" and then immediately became perfect. Having done according to his express desire, Elēlasingan observed that the crows and other animals which devoured his holy flesh became beautiful as gold; and therefore, greatly wondering, he built a temple, and instituted worship, on the spot where the sacred corpse had lain.

CURAL.

I.—The Praise of God.

1. Eternal God all things precedes,
   As Alpha all the letters leads.
2. The learning's vain that does not fall
   At His good feet Who knoweth all.
3. His feet their flowers of thought among
   Who joy to feel, shall flourish long.
4. Who hold His feet Who neither knows
   To long nor loathe, avoid all woes.
5. God's praise who tell, are free from right
   And wrong, the twins of dreaming night.
6. They prosper evermore who keep
   His law in Whom the senses sleep.
7. His feet, Whose likeness none can find,
   Alone can ease the anxious mind.
8. Who swims the sea of vice is he
   Who clasps the feet of Virtue's Sea.
9. Like palsied sense, no head's complete
   That bows not at Perfection's feet.
10. They only pass, of all who swim,
    The sea of births, who cleave to Him.

II.—The Value of Rain.

11. The genial rain ambrosia call :
The world but lasts while rain shall fall.
12. 'Tis rain begets the food we eat :
The precious rain is drink and meat.
13. Let clouds their visits stay, and dearth
Distresses all the sea-girt earth.
14. Unless the fruitful shower descend
The ploughman's sacred toil must end.
15. Refraining, rain destroys ; and then,
Propitious, calls to life again.
16. If from the cloud no drop appear,
No grassy blade its head will rear.
17. Except the cloud its stores repay,
The ocean's wealth will waste away.
18. The gods would find this world deny
Due off'rings 'neath a barren sky.
19. Were heaven above to fail, below
Nor alms nor penance earth would show.
20. Since without water, without rain
Life's duties were essay'd in vain.

III.—The Excellence of Ascetics.

21. No boasted greatness is so high
As theirs, who self by rule deny.

22. As soon you'll count the dead, as tell
How much ascetics all excel.

23. No lustre can with theirs compare
Who know the right, and virtue wear.

24. With hook of firmness to restrain *
The senses five, is heaven to gain.

25. How great their power who hold such sway,
Indra, heaven's King, himself must say.†

26. What's difficult the great will do :
The small will paths of ease pursue.

27. The world is theirs, the bounds who tell
Of taste, sight, feeling, sound, and smell.

28. Full-worded men, by what they say,
Their greatness to the world display.

29. Their wrath who've climb'd the mount of good,
Though transient, cannot be withstood.

30. With even kindness cloth'd tow'rds all,
The Beautiful ‡ the virtuous call.

IV.—The Power of Virtue.

31. None greater good than virtue know,
Whence heaven and various riches flow.

32. Who follow it have highest gain ;
Who shun it, deepest loss and pain.

* As the hook guides the elephant.

† The allusion is to his suffering from Gautama's curse.

‡ Anthanar, a title of the Brahmans, their exclusive right to which is thus disputed.

33. To practise it be all your strife,
The ceaseless aim and rule of life.

34. In purity of mind 't is found,
Not outward show, and empty sound.

35. Four things t' eschew does virtue teach,
Ill-will, lust, wrath, and angry speech.

36. Your friend without delay if made,
In death 't will be your deathless aid.

37. Needless are words : its power is seen
Outside and in the palankeen.*

38. With no lost days for which t' atone,
'Gainst threat'ning births it rears a stone.

39. Nor joy can spring, nor praise can rise,
But in the pleasure it supplies.

40. Virtue is what ought to be done,
And vice what every one should shun.

V.—The Domestic State.

41. The worthy householder is he
Who aids the holy orders three.†

42. His help the poor and pious share,
And they who die attract his care.

* The lack of virtue in a former birth makes one man a palankeen-bearer, whilst its reward to another who practised it is that he is carried in the palankeen.

† The student (Bramachari), the married hermit (Vānaprastan), and the lonely anchorite (Sanniyāsi).

43. Chief praise the five-fold duty earns,
Which ghosts, God, guests, kin, self concerns.
44. Who dare no wrong, and food bestow,
Their house is strong, their seed shall grow.
45. Domestic life its end and gain
Enjoys, where love and virtue reign.
46. Who virtuous married life will flee
To turn a monk,—what profits he?
47. He who adorns the married state
Is head of all whose aims are great.
48. Pilgrim himself, with double load,
He others helps in virtue's road.
49. Marriage is virtue; though the same
Is hermit-life, when free from blame.
50. On earth such wedded bliss who prove,
In heaven among the gods shall move.

VI.—The Worth of a Help-meet.

51. Her husband's means her law of life,
Who fits the house,—she is the wife.
52. The greatness of the married state
The wife is, or it is not great.
53. What is there not, when she's complete?
What is there, when she is not meet?
54. On what may more esteem be placed
Than faithful woman firmly chaste?
55. Instead of God, who worship pays
Her spouse, says "Rain," and heaven obeys.

56. True wives unwearied shrink from blame,
Their husbands cherish, and their fame.

57. Of what avail are prisons barr'd?
Their chastity is women's guard.

58. If women wifely bliss obtain,
Great joy where dwell the gods they gain.

59. With ill-famed wives, whom men deride,—
Not theirs the lion-step of pride.

60. With jewels of good children dress'd,
Whose wives are blameless,—they are bless'd.

VII.—Obtaining Sons.

61. The world no greater good supplies
Than offspring virtuous and wise.

62. Who such unequall'd treasures own,
Beneath no vengeful fortunes groan.

63. The virtues of their children bring
New wealth to that from which they spring.

64. The rice is all ambrosial made
In which their tiny hands have play'd.

65. Their contact gives a blissful thrill:
Their notes the soul with sweetness fill.

66. Whose little ones ne'er prattled near,
May say, "The lute delights the ear."

67. A father's blessing is, to 'enthrone
Amid the circling wise his son.

68. With yearning pride his bosom swells,
Because his boy himself excels.

69. His mother hears confess'd his worth,
And triumphs more than at his birth.
70. He loves his sire, who wakes the strain,
"What penance such a son could gain?"

VIII.—LOVINGKINDNESS.

71. What bolt holds love? One starting tear
Wakes show'rs from answering eyelids dear.
72. Their bones the loving do not call
Their own: who love not, grasp at all.
73. From love did virtue gain its worth
To win the matchless human birth.
74. Love makes the lov'd desire, and hence
Springs friendship's boundless excellence.
75. Heaven's bliss, and married joy below,
From love with virtue mated flow.
76. Love is not virtue's friend alone:
To vice its screening power is known.
77. Worms shrivel in the solar blaze;
So justice the unloving slays.
78. Whose minds to love afford no room,
Like wither'd trees in deserts bloom.
79. From outward grace they nothing win,
Who want the charms of love within.
80. Whose life is not by love inspired
Are skeletons in skin attired.

IX.—HOSPITALITY.

81. Of keeping house the sacred end
Is, guests with kindly care to tend.

82. Though food of endless life you eat,
To shut the guest out is not meet.

83. The house that honours guests each day,
In trouble shall not waste away.

84. Gladsome prosperity shall rest
Where smiles reçẹive the worthy guest.

85. Need seed in that man's field be sown,
Whose caller's meal precedes his own?

86. Guest after guest, who waits to see,
A welcome guest in heaven shall be.

87. The good thus gain'd can no one count:
The pilgrims' worth is its amount.

88. Inhospitable souls shall say,
"We've held our wealth, and have no stay."

89. Rich dullards who no alms bestow,
Shall want amidst abundance know.

90. As fades the flower * when smelt, the guest
Is by averted looks depress'd.

X.—AFFABILITY.

91. Sweet words and guileless gently flow
From lips of those who duty know.

* The fabulous *anitcham*, dying when only smelled, without being touched.

92. To give with genererous heart cheers less
Than smiling face and sweet address.
93. Virtue is, issuing from the mind,
Sweet words, with dulcet looks combined.
94. Sweet speech that growing gladness yields
From penury woe-working shields.
95. He is adorn'd, and he alone,
Who humbly speaks, with courteous tone.
96. His sins decrease, his virtue grows,
Who alms with pleasant words bestows.
97. The cheerful word and kindly deed
To righteousness and merit lead.
98. Sweet speech, that shows itself sincere,
Hereafter pleasure brings, and here.
99. How can he utter words that sting,
Who sees what sweets from sweet words spring?
100. With sweet words near, who harsh words try,
Eat fruit that's sour, when ripe is nigh.

XI.—GRATITUDE.

101. For nothing had, assistance given
In worth surpasses earth and heaven.
102. Favours bestow'd in time of need,
Though small, the spacious world exceed.
103. What's right, not what his gain will be,
Who weighs, his gift outweighs the sea.
104. A help as seed of millet small,
Who finds it, counts a palm-tree tall.

105. The worth of those to whom 't is shown
Measures the favour, not its own.
106. Cling to your faultless friends, and those
Whose kindness was your staff in woes.
107. Through seven-fold births in mind should stay
Their love who sorrow wiped away.
108. Forgetting goodness is not good:
'T is wrong o'er wrongs at all to brood.
109. Thŏugh cruel now, who once were kind
For favours done will favour find.
110. Who slay all virtues death may fly:
Who obligations kill must die.

XII.—Equity.

111. That only will for virtue pass
Which fits itself to every class.
112. The just man's store secure remains,
And happy children reap his gains.
113. If right be absent, turn away
From tempting good without delay.
114. Who just and who unjust have been
Is plainly in their offspring seen.
115. Since loss and gain not causeless rise,
A temper smooth adorns the wise.
116. "I perish," let him think, whose mind
From justice turns, to sin inclined.
117. The man is rich, the world can see,
Who dwells in honest poverty.

118. The great, like balance poised, are fair,—
Justice the ornament they wear.

119. Justice will crooked thoughts disown,
Not crookedness of speech alone.

120. Like his, the trader true delights
To guard his neighbour's goods and rights.

XIII.—SELF-CONTROL.

121. Self-rule to the immortals tends :
Its want in densest darkness ends.

122. A treasure to be kept with care,
No gains with self-restraint compare.

123. Who self-control true knowledge deem,
And practise it, command esteem.

124. Adhering to their proper state,
They rise above the mountain great.

125. Though good for all, the wealthy gain
In humbleness the richest vein.

126. One birth keep in the senses five,
Like tortoise, through the seven to thrive.

127. If nothing else, the tongue restrain :
Unruly talkers suffer pain.

128. One sinful word, its power so strong,
Turns good to bad, and right to wrong.

129. A burn will heal, but festering stays
The wound a burning tongue conveys.

130. Virtue will watch their steps to bless
Who anger and desire suppress.

XIV.—BEHAVIOUR.

131. Since conduct good will greatness give,
Care less for life than how you live.

132. In many ways though you excel,
This crowning aid be guarded well.

133. Good birth in life correct is seen:
Low living brings the birth that's mean.

134. Priests lore forgot again may know,
But forfeit caste by living low.

135. For wealth as envy vainly sighs,
So men ill-manner'd cannot rise.

136. The wise from order will not stray,
But shun their guilt who disobey.

137. While greatness from right conduct grows,
Disgrace alone from evil flows.

138. Behaviour good is virtue's seed;
But endless griefs from ill proceed.

139. Though memory fail, by rule who walk
Still keep their tongues from sinful talk.

140. Their learning's vain, who do not know
How smoothly with the world to go.

XV.—PURITY.

141. The blind to right and rights alone
Desire to have whom others own.

142. Outside the law, no fool's so great
As stands outside his neighbour's gate.

143. No better than the dead he lives
Who foul offence to friendship gives.

144. No boasted qualities protect
The wretch by thought of sin uncheck'd.

145. The guilt made light of yet will stay:
The fault will never fade away.

146. Hatred, sin, fear, and shame,—these four
Are with th' adulterer evermore.

147. The lust by virtue is abhorr'd
For one who has her lawful lord.

148. He only leads a manly life
Who looks not on another's wife.

149. To whom, in all the sea-girt earth,
Comes good, but men of moral worth?

150. All other vice inflicts less loss
Than lust a neighbour's fence to cross.

XVI.—PATIENCE.

151. As earth its diggers, they who bear
The scornful, show a virtue rare.

152. There's greatness in enduring ill:
Forgetting it is greater still.

153. As poorest they who beggars shun,
Who suffer fools—so strong are none.

154. Who patience practises with pains,
Unsulled excellence retains.

155. In no esteem the hasty hold:
The patient prize as hidden gold.

156. A day, and passion's joy is pass'd :
Patience is praised while earth shall last.
157. From hurting cruel foes refrain :
'Twere pity to increase their pain.
158. A man by patience may o'erthrow
In evil work who farthest go.
159. Who meekly wicked words endure
Than saints ascetic are more pure.
160. Who 're patient when reproach is cast,
Excel in greatness those who fast.

XVII.—AGAINST ENVY.

161. Esteem'd like good behaviour be
A character from envy free.
162. No acquisition can be won
Above the power of envying none.
163. Another's gains who envious views,
Nor virtue he, nor wealth pursues.
164. Since woes the way of evil throng,
From envy practise nothing wrong.
165. No outward foes need arts employ :
Envy suffices to destroy.
166. Who envies such as gifts receive,
For kindred, clothes, and food shall grieve.
167. Repell'd by envy, Lakshmi * starts,
Presents her sister,† and departs.

* Goddess of Prosperity. † Mūdēvi, goddess of Adversity.

168. Envy will wealth on earth dispel,
And lead the soul to fiery hell.

169. Envy made rich, uprightness brought
To poverty, were theme for thought!

170. The envious never great were seen:
The free from envy never mean.

XVIII.—AGAINST COVETOUSNESS.

171. The covetous their houses doom
To ruin, and the guilt assume.

172. Who shrink from gainful sin with shame,
Will nothing do deserving blame.

173. For better joy to come who long,
For trifling pleasure do no wrong.

174. Set free from sin and sense's chain,
The wise, though poor, content remain.

175. Superior knowledge meets no meed,
That acts tow'rds all with maudlin greed.

176. His seeming path to grace, in pain
Shall end, who evil does for gain.

177. The fruit of covetousness shun:
In all its gain there's glory none.

178. Wealth's permanence in this is known,—
Not coveting what others own.

179. To bless in virtue's way the wise
Who covet nothing, Lakshmi flies.

180. Contentment's greatness conquers all:
The reckless greedy ruined fall.

XIX.—AGAINST BACKBITING.

181. For one who wide from virtue strays,
"He does not backbite" is some praise.
182. Who present smile, and absent curse,
Than virtue's enemies are worse.
183. 'Twere greater good by far to die,
Than live to backbite and to lie.
184. Though careless words you present say,
Yet speak with caution when away.
185. Who loves to backbite, makes it clear
In virtue's praise he 's insincere.
186. His failings will be search'd and shown,
Who makes another's failings known.
187. While foolish slanders friends divide,
By laughter-making words they 're tied.
188. What will they not to strangers do,
Who faults of friends expose to view?
189. Earth bears in charity their weight
Who of the absent basely prate.
190. As others' faults, if men their own
Would see, what evil would be known?

XX.—AGAINST PROFITLESS CONVERSATION.

191. With useless words who numbers grieves
Deserv'd contempt from all receives.
192. Vain talk that many ears offends,
Is worse that vicious deeds tow'rds friends.

193. The babbler's useless lips proclaim
That "Good-for-nothing" is his name.
194. Who deals in light offensive speech,
Nor virtue keeps, nor right can reach.
195. If things of nought good people say,
Their reputation flies away.
196. Whose worth in weightless words is shown,
As chaff of men, not man be known.
197. If nonsense you will speak, so do:
The wise will scorn to follow you.
198. The sage, who seek the highest gain,
From words of little use refrain.
199. For pointless talk, they will not see
Even in forgetfulness, a plea.
200. To purpose speak, whenever heard,
And never say an empty word.

XXI.—Fear of Sin.

201. Who virtue's honours humbly win,
Not sinners, fear the pride of sin.
202. Dread wickedness, as fire your dread:
Sin leads to sin, as flames are spread.
203. Foremost of all the wise are those
Who will not hurt their very foes.
204. Virtue his ruin plots who plans
In thoughtless thought another man's.
205. Who sinning makes "I'm poor" his plea,
Shall afterwards much poorer be.

206. Who'd not have pain himself pursue,
Let him no ill to others do.

207. Men spite of other foes may live,
But sin its deadly blow will give.

208. Destruction, as their shadow true,
The steps of sinners will pursue.

209. Let none who loves himself at all
Do any sin, however small.

210. Know ye he's from destruction freed,
Who turns to do no evil deed.

XXII.—BENEVOLENCE.

211. The kind seek nothing back again :
What from the world do clouds obtain ?

212. The aim of toil, of wealth the end,
Is want to help, and worth befriend.

213. 'Tis hard in either world to find
A greater good than being kind.

214. He lives, whose life in love is led :
Another, reckon with the dead.

215. The brimming tank the town supplies :
So wealth is order'd by the wise.

216. Who gladly of their plenty give
Like ripening fruit-trees with us live.

217. Diseases and distress they cure,
Like plants of healing virtue sure.

218. Their sense of duty will not cease
From kindness, though their wealth decrease.

219. The good man's poverty and grief
Is wanting power to give relief.
220. Of loss by bounty ne'er complain,
But sell yourself such loss to gain.

XXIII.—ALMSGIVING.

221. They give who give to helpless need:
Not they whose gifts to getting lead.
222. A good way call'd, still begging's bad:
To give is good, were heaven not had.
223. 'Tis giving argues noble birth,
Not pleading "I am nothing worth."
224. Not sweet are calls for charity,
Until the beggar's smile we see.
225. Higher the power which hunger cures,
Than penance which its pangs endures.
226. Removing hunger, who sustains
The poor, makes room to hoard his gains.
227. Who's wont his food around to part
Is safe from hunger's burning smart.
228. Do they who, hard-eyed, save to waste,
Not know what joys the generous taste?
229. To beg itself is greater joy
Than appetite alone to cloy.
230. Joyless as death is nought: yet this
Compared with selfishness is bliss.

XXIV.—FAME.

231. They live with praise who freely give,
And profit most of all that live.

232. His lasting praise no voice but shows,
One alms who on the poor bestows.

233. 'Gainst ruin proof there's nothing known
Save fame, that towering stands alone.

234. From praising gods the god-world turns
To praise the man who praises earns.

235. The famous flourish in decay,
And none in dying live but they.

236. If praise may not this life adorn,
'Twere better never to be born.

237. How without pain can they remain
Who, praised by none, their censors pain?

238. All own it shame to end our days,
And leave no progeny of praise.

239. The ground will lose its fertile name,
That bears a body void of fame.

240. They live who live above disgrace:
They're not alive whose life is base.

Life of Ouvvay.

AS might be expected, the list of Tamil sages is not adorned by many female names. Yet four learned ladies, excelled by few of the prouder sex, have handed valued writings down to the present day. SUDICODUTTA NAYCHIYAR was a foundling brought up by a Vaishnava devotee. Zealously consecrating herself to the service of her foster-father's god, she composed the works entitled *Tiruppavay* and *Tirumorlyi.* PUNITHAVATI, a merchant's daughter early married, was deserted by her husband, who took another wife. As he withstood all advances made with a view to reconciliation, she assumed the habit of an ascetic, repaired to the Imaus, and there died. Among other productions, she left the *Atputhattiruvanthathi*, a poem in high repute with the Saiva sect. SANPAGAVADIVI was the daughter of one of the handmaids of a Chōla rajah. Captivated by her genius, King Carical adopted her, while she was yet a child, into the royal family, giving the precocious lady a splendid mansion and an imposing retinue. The fame of her maturing charms attracted numerous suitors; but, above prejudice and beyond reproach, having resolved not to marry any one who could not overcome her in poetical conflict, she exulted in remaining single and unvanquished till her twenty-fifth year. Then she was proved to be not invincible. The professors of Madura, whom she had characterized as a senate of dunces, being unable to endure her scorn any longer, their doughty president Narkira put on the disguise of a wood-seller, and himself encountered the beautiful boaster. The combatants mercilessly assailed each other with poetic enigmas, all of them preserved, until, after a severe and protracted struggle, the head of the university discomfited and led captive the damsel.

The fourth excellent lady, whose life we have now to trace, is the queen of female sages. Indeed, among Tamil writers, OUVVAY is second to none but Tiru-Valluvar. It is greatly to be lamented that her biography is not less absurd and varnished than that of her illustrious brother. She is a distinguished proof that the garden of knowledge was not always forbidden ground to virtuous daughters of India, and that they formerly enjoyed more social liberty than in the present day. It must of course be remembered that she was of low caste on her mother's side. But it is clear, from the traditions respecting her character and conduct, and from the writings in which she speaks to successive generations, that it would be wrong to pronounce her a temple-woman. Hindus get easily over the difficulty by referring to the Deity within her; but to matter-of-fact Europeans it is evident that genius, watched by the eye of restraint, and fed with the oil of perseverance, a brilliant human flame, was the divinity in possession.

Ouvvay, a new-born babe, was discovered by a minstrel in a choultry neary Urayūr; and, as she grew up, she fared very well among the Pānars, a class, now nearly extinct, of musicians and singers, whose office was to wait upon kings and pronounce their praises. She is supposed to have been an incarnation of Sarasvati, Brahma's consort, who, as the goddess of music, poetry, and learning, knew well, we may be sure, with whom to choose her habitation. Wherever she went, her lips breathed piety and wisdom, and her hand wrote moral verses and proverbs. She was a benefactress to all who needed her blessings; and it is said that she wrought miracles, healing diseases, converting base things into gold, and mixing the medicine of immortality. People of every caste welcomed and honoured the marvellous woman.

The use of surnames merely titular and descriptive in their origin, is peculiar to no age or country. Hebrew appellations of the kind will occur at once to the reader's memory. Familiar names among ourselves are Greathead, Armstrong, Scattergood, Shakespear, Sheepshanks, and the like. We know who was the Iron Duke, and who the Little Corporal. The people of India are wont to give telling titles to individuals. An English general was called by them The Devil's Brother. Three missionary colleagues were distinguished, the youngest as The Tall Padre, the next as The Short Padre, and, in an honourable sense, the oldest as The Great Padre. It has already been remarked that, the Tamil poets not having been accustomed to affix their names to their writings, several of them are known to posterity by only their acquired titles. Take a few examples. One is called Ashdavathani, from the retentiveness of his memory; and another Curlyangayar, from his crippled hand, injured by a red-hot iron which he had been compelled to seize when on trial by ordeal. As we have seen, the real name of the chief of Tamil poets, Tiru-Valluvar, has long been forgotten. So the next most famous of the seven kindred sages bears the name of OUVVAY, OR THE ELDERLY LADY. She was also called "*Curlyuccupadi*," or *She who sang for a meal.* For this title she was indebted to the vanity of a dancing-girl, Silambi of Ambal, and the churlishness of the poet Cambar. Silambi had offered the versifier five-hundred *pons** for a metrical inscription to her praise and glory. That being only half the price he took for such a stanza, he inscribed with charcoal but half a verse on the wall of her dwelling, and then wickedly departed. Fortunately Ouvvay called immediately, and for merely a dish of rice defeated the rhymester's

* A coin, valued at 3*s*. 6*d*. sterling.

object, and removed the girl's perplexity, completing the inscription as follows :—

"Of rivers the best is Cāvery, and Chōla all kings
surpasses,
Of lands his are the richest, and the comeliest of
lasses—
Is Silambi of Ambal, and no silambu's * so sweet
As the golden one soft tinkling upon her lotus-feet."

Ouvvay once honoured with a visit the island of Ceylon, where for a succession of days it rains twice a year, and where it never rains but it pours. Caught in the torrent, she took shelter in the dwelling of two women of low caste; and Angavay and Sangavay treated her with so much kindness that she rewarded them with the promise,—"I will cause you to be given in marriage to the divine King of Tirucovalur." Remembering her word, she waited upon the rajah, and commended to him her friends. His majesty replied,—"If Chēran, Chōlan, and Pandiyan give me these women in marriage, I will receive them forthwith." Whereupon she addressed the following invocation to the god of wisdom and enterprise, and of marriage rites :—

"O son of him who joys to wear
The tiger's skin,† and made thee bear

* A foot ornament. † Siva.

The elephant's huge head, appear;
Reveal thy fragrant presence here;
And swiftly by my fingers write,
And make this leaf the kings invite.
Thou double-tusk'd one, heed my will;
Thou single-handed, show thy skill;
Or she who breathes this pious verse
Will vex thee with her venom'd curse."

Pillayar readily vouchsafed his aid; and she inscribed the charmed invitation on an *ola* or palmyra-leaf, folded it up, and despatched it, by the god of the winds, to the three kings. When they had read it, they proceeded without delay to a marriage saloon called into existence for the occasion by Ouvvay's power; and, on their arrival, they thus addressed her:—"Mother, here is a piece of palmyra wood: if you make it become a tree, put forth leaves, and produce its young fruit, and will present to us each a specimen, we will do as you desire." Consenting, she lifted up her voice, and sang,—

"Before the palace-like saloon,
Umbrellas silvery as the moon
The bridegroom's royal friends reveal,
Who come with holy oil to seal
Their happy fate, whose shelt'ring roof
Render'd the stranger tempest-proof,

But first command, my claims to show,
This lifeless wood be made to grow.
So let the shell-white sprout be seen,
Unfold its leaves of deep'ning green,
And form its fruit, till ripe there fall
For each his black and ruddy ball."

Her song concluded, they beheld their request literally fulfilled. Each held in his hand the round red-tinged fruit. There was no alternative. Ouvvay having complied with their requirement, they, trembling with awe, hastened to comply with her's, and gave the two women away in marriage to the divine king of Tirucovalur.

When Valluvar went up with his *Cural* to the Madura College, Ouvvay, his worthy companion, was not to be put to shame by the assembled sages. In spite of the maxim, if then in vogue, "Talking by gesture is improper for women," she asked the professors to explain, if they could, certain signs she made. Not satisfied with their answers, she became her own interpreter, and thus gave the dumb actions a voice:—

"Bestowing alms, in virtue live:
Though but a pinch of rice, yet give
  Before you eat your own:
The five great sins will pass away,
When power you get to know and say
  That God is One alone."

"The Hindu system of moral philosophy involves four questions, viz. :—What is virtue, and how is it to be exercised? What is wealth, and how is it to be acquired? What is pleasure, and how is it to be enjoyed? What is heavenly bliss, and how is it to be obtained?" Valluvar in his *Cural* treated formally only the first three questions. The fourth was not unapproached by him, but anticipated, being included, as Todittalay-Virlyuttandinār, one of the Madura judges, pronounced, in his discussion of the three preceding topics. But Ouvvay, on learning the construction of the poem, thought her brother liable to censure; and, to show how easy a task he had undertaken, she "compressed all the four questions, and their answers," in one impromptu stanza, which may thus be rendered :—

"Virtue's giving without halt;
Wealth is getting without fault;
Pleasure is the quenchless flame
Blending two with tastes the same;
Giving, getting, loving nought,
Gathering all the power of thought,
Losing self in the abyss,
Searching God, is heavenly bliss."

Ouvvay knew how to acknowledge merit, and to rebuke pretence. As she chanced one day to be sitting on the ground with her feet outstretched in a street of Urayūr, Culōtunga the Chōla king came along, with Ottaycūtar, who was one of his poets, and Pugarlyēnthi, also a poet, but of the Pandiya court. As the monarch went by, the old lady withdrew one of her feet; and as the Madura poet Pugarlyēnthi passed, she retracted the other. To Ottaycūtar, who came next, she must surely pay some equal mark of respect. On the contrary, as if he were nobody, she made haste to stretch out both her legs again. The offended gentleman desired an explanation. She said, "I drew back one foot for the king, because he wears the crown; and both feet for Pugarlyēnthi, because he is a great poet; but I have not withdrawn either of my feet for you, as you are nothing but a dunce. If you are as able as Pugarlyēnthi, prove it by improvising a verse in which, while you praise the Chōla country and its king, the word *mathi* shall occur three times." The said word, signifying *the moon* and *wit*, only coming twice in his laboured stanza, she asked with concern, "Where is thy other wit?" He was so ashamed, that he could give no answer. She then applied to Pugarlyēnthi, only politely suggesting that he should substitute the Pandiya kingdom; and Ottaycūtar was outdone by the more ready poet of Madura. She applauded him, and tried him with another word, in the use of which he was equally successful.

Like other reputable women, Ouvvay was slightly inconsistent and eccentric. Declaring in favour of marriage, yet she remained single. She could speak disparagingly of her own sex; but could come to their rescue, when her heart was wounded. Hearing some lords of creation reviling the character of the ladies, she turned upon them with the impromptu :—

"All women are good, if let alone,—
They are spoilt by those who rule them;
And by men might a little sense be shown,
But the women so befool them."

Tradition says that this distinguished poetess reached the age of two hundred and forty years, and then voluntarily retired from earth. She selected, as her final engagement below, the worship of the wise and powerful god whom she had once threatened to curse. Pillayar found it necessary to demand why she, who had never offered worship in a slovenly manner before, now went through it hurriedly. Mentioning the names of two sages, she answered, "Swamy, they are going to Kailasam, and desire my company." "I will get you there before them," said the benignant deity; "only finish your ceremonies in your usual style." The believing woman did so; and with his gentle trunk Pillayar lifted her to Siva's heaven. On their arrival, her two friends, to their amazement, found Ouvvay already in Kailasam. By a plainer account, "according to the custom of her times, she made the *mahāprasthāna-*

gamana, or great journey to the Imaus, and died there."

The compositions attributed to Ouvvay have received unmeasured commendation. Mr. S. C. Chitty thinks that, advancing farther in her researches and teaching, she "was more keen and clever than even her brother." * Beschi pronounced her "moral sentences worthy of Seneca himself." † The Rev. Peter Percival regards her works as "of great beauty and value, replete with lessons of wisdom;" and affirms that they "have never been surpassed for sententious brevity, and generally are equally distinguished by purity of principle." ‡ Another critic says, "She sang like Sappho, yet not of love, but of virtue." § Thirteen books are ascribed to her:—*Nigandu*, a dictionary of materia medica; *Panthananthathi*, a panegyric on Panthan, a wealthy merchant of Caveripatnam; *Nyana-Cural*, a treatise on mataphysics; and the ten following on ethics and religion, *Tarisanapattu*, *Arunthamirlmalay*, *Nanmarnicovay*, *Nannutcovay*, *Asathicovay*, *Calviyorlyuccam*, *Nalvarlyi*, *Condayventhan*, *Attisudi*, and *Muthuray*.

The most important are the five named last, of which three are given in the following pages. Like all the rest, they are composed in the high language; and some of the sentences they contain are ambiguous

* Tamil Plutarch. † Introduction to Shen-Tamil Grammar.
‡ Land of the Vēda. § Calcutta Review.

even to learned natives. They are often, therefore, altogether above the comprehension of little children. Every missionary verifies the statement of a distinguished chaplain:—"A short time before I left Madras, I went into one of the native schools, and requested the teacher to let me see what the boys were reading. He showed me some *olas*, on which were written the sayings of Ouvvay. I desired him to explain them to me; when he took up another *ola*, which contained the interpretation, and began to read. I stopped him, saying that I wished him to tell me from his own mind what he supposed to be the sense of the proverbs, or even of the written interpretation. Upon this, he looked in my face, and confessed, with a smile, that he understood neither the one nor the other. Such is the ignorance of most of the native schoolmasters; and it is evident that their scholars can derive no moral benefit whatever from repeating sentences, however sound the morality they contain, unless they are made to comprehend their meaning and application." * Yet Ouvvay's sayings seem to have been originally prepared chiefly for the young; and certain it is that they are among the first, as well as the best, books put into the hands and heads of the people of Southern India. Commentaries, as intimated above, are attached to some of them; and the living teacher, not always

* Hough's Reply.

quite so incompetent as the schoolmaster referred to, vouchsafes his explanations. But it is quite the Hindu system to store the memory with pregnant words, leaving the fruit of them, gradually appearing under the maturing influences of thought and time, to be gathered by the judgment in after days.

There is not a purer composition among all the standards of India than Ouvvay's *Muthuray*, or *Thirty Aphorisms*, frequently called also, from the first words of the dedication, *Vakkundam.* This book, the first of The Elderly Lady's which we give, is of the greater importance from the fact that missionaries, not only have not excluded it from their schools, but have themselves given editions of it to their pupils and to the world. It is found, for instance, in the *Fifth Instructor*, published by the Jaffna missionaries, but in the missionary edition, besides the substitution of another dedication or introduction, the arrangement of the stanzas is entirely changed; there is an omission of the 27th, without substitution; and for the 3rd, 7th, 18th, 22nd, 23rd, and 29th, there are introduced stanzas from other sources, including two from Ouvvay's *Nalvarlyi.* Is it well, even if it could be shown that they are called for on moral grounds, to take such liberties with the reputed writings of a celebrated sage? If the anxiety of the missionaries to withhold pernicious aliment may be commended, let the impossibility of their doing so by such means be not forgotten. Omitted verses are easily and invariably supplied, even in Christian schools, from original copies in the possession of the children, or by the too willing native teachers. Nothing can be gained for the truth by endeavouring to make a pagan writer shine in other than Pagan colours. Moreover, missionaries thus expose themselves to the charge of fraud and imposition. It may be urged in their defence that perhaps they arranged their edition from conflicting *ola* copies before the press in the service of native editors had fixed the text. Otherwise, how could they shut out the 18th, 22nd, 23rd, and 27th stanzas, while retaining the 5th, 19th, and 20th?

Have not the missionaries taken needless and inconsistent trouble in editing and printing books of this order for the purposes of education? A time may come when such volumes may be handled by them in their seminaries with impunity; but at present, important as it is to recognize and honour truth in whatever associations found, and desirable as it seems to conciliate the people by paying all possible respect to their treasured literature, the propriety of using the productions of native authors as class-books in missionary institutions, steeped with heathenism as the best of them are, is seriously questionable. Let the Church place such books, if they must be in possession, where the Government of Continental India—not that of Ceylon—deposits the Holy Bible, only on the shelves of school libraries. Haste without speed is not so good as slowness with safety and ultimate success. Ouvvay's works themselves, some of them the most excellent of Tamil writings, repeated by the lips of all the rising generation in the North of Ceylon and the South of Hindustan, suffice to show the necessity of Christian school-books and other useful publications in the native languages. The thought is mournful that, even in mission seminaries, for more than half a century, along with her lessons of profound wisdom, she has been left to teach the children to believe, like their fathers, in a blind fate, in a succession of dependent births, in the servile subordination of her sex, and in idolatry. Granted that her sayings are wonderfully correct and moral for a heathen writer, they are not pure and true enough for Christian teaching. Difficult as many, particularly young people, find it to understand some of her sentences, and to appreciate their literary excellence, yet the paganism dwelling in her writings reveals itself readily to babes.

Next follows the *Attisudi*, a title taken from the first words of its dedication to Pillayar or Ganapathi. The original sentences being arranged, like the lines or stanzas of twelve of the Hebrew poems in the sacred volume, in the order of their initial letters, some have called it *The Golden Alphabet* of the Tamils. The same title might be claimed for other collections of moral sentences. Only 108 letters are thus honoured in the *Attisudi;* whereas, exclusive of the Grandonic or Sanscrit characters used in addition to them, the Tamil letters and their combinations amount to 247. Our alphabet not being lengthy enough to stand at the beginnings of the aphorisms, they may be arranged in English

> "With rhymes like watchmen standing at the close,
> To keep the verse from running into prose."

The *Conday-vēnthan*, another book of proverbs, likewise takes its title from the opening word of the brief invocation. Here again the arrangement is alphabetical. Yet not so many letters are recognized as in the *Attisudi;* and, on the other hand, one is honoured which is passed over in that golden alphabet. The *Attisudi* is hortatory and imperative, the *Conday-vēnthan* indicative and aphoristic. Its third line is quoted by a Tamil writer in the following verse, which serves to show in what esteem Ouvvay is held in India :—"Ye dispute vainly among yourselves, O sages, when ye say that among the four established orders of life this or that is to be preferred, and deceive yourselves: our revered mother, who was herself a manifestation of virtue, has said,—'No virtue is more excellent than the virtue of domestic life.'" *

To these translations, as the fittest place in the volume, though not a work of "our revered mother," is appended the *Garland of Advice for Women.* This little

* Ellis's Cural.

book is interesting, because it is intended exclusively for females, recommends Ouvvay's maxims to their observance, and is found in the hands and lips of not a few girls in the Tamil districts. What in England would be regretted as forwardness, is applauded as wisdom in India. The translator remembers a native friend speaking with admiration of a child who, when a case of frailty was being discussed in a village assembly, had settled the question, to his astonishment and that of all present, by quoting from the *Garland* a precept which the reader would think altogether unbecoming in the mouth of a little maid. UMAPATHI is the name of the author. The composition appears to be comparatively modern. At the end of every line is a word equivalent to "My girl" or "my dear." It is another golden alphabet, and may be compared with that in the Holy Bible containing the description of a good wife, in "the words of King Lemuel, the prophecy that his mother taught him."

MUTHURAY.

Who statedly with floral gifts attend,
Before the trunk-faced red-one's * footstool bend,
And pious homage reverently pay,
Shall from the goddess lotus-throned † acquire
Wit, eloquence, and all that they desire,
And never sink in bodily decay.

---

1. If suffering worth to acts of kindness move,
Dismiss the fear your bounty may not prove
A source at last of profit and delight :
The water furnish'd to its early root,
In sweeter draughts from future plenteous fruit
The cocoa's crown will gratefully requite. ‡

2. The valued favours the deserving gain
Like sculptures in eternal rock remain ;
Of virtue's tribute charity is sure :
But vain is kindness to the worthless shown,
Who debts and duties evermore disown ;
On water written words as well endure.

* Ganapathi. † Lakshmi.

‡ The young cocoa-nut tree needs copious and frequent watering. The fluid of its fresh fruit is a pleasant and abundant drink.

3. When senseless grief the live-long day englooms,
In vain attractively the garden blooms ;
In vain the spouseless maid her beauty wears :
So youth when needy is a tiresome stage,
And wealth but misery in helpless age,
A bitter mockery of peevish cares.

4. To love, though loved, the callous base ne'er learn ;
But love for love the good and wise return ;
Their greatness through calamities remains ;
A purer whiteness as the sea-shell shows,
When fiercely the containing furnace glows ;
As seething milk its flavour still retains.

5. Although in foliage richly dress'd they rise,
In figure faultless, and mature in size,
As trees no fruit except in season bear,
In any project sooner to succeed,
And gain the end before the time decreed,
Nor wealth avails, nor toil, nor wakeful care.

6. Not softly yielding as the building towers,
Not bending gently when the load o'erpowers,
The stony column will asunder fly :
So they who scorn their honour to survive
'Gainst overwhelming adversaries strive,
Refusing homage though they muster nigh.

7. The depth and surface of the pool decide
The growth and limit of the lily's pride :
So erudition is on study based ;

So riches show accumulated worth
By penance purchased in a previous birth;
  So character from son to sire is traced.

8. Happy the eyes that on the pious rest,
The ears that hear their useful words are bless'd,
  And bless'd the lips that all their virtues tell;
More happy they, their character who wear,
Their friendship gain, their reputation share,
  Their sacred paths frequent, and with them dwell.

9. The very sight of wicked men is ill,
Their graceless words the ear with evil fill,
  The lips with risk their attributes portray,
And 'tis the height of self-inflicted wrong
To mingle with their sin-infectious throng,
  Attend their cursed steps, and with them stay.

10. The water turn'd to where the rice-crop grows
Refreshes kindly, as it thither flows,
  The common grass that in its channel lies:
In every age, the genial rains that fall
To cheer the good, are shared alike by all,
  And virtue's revenue the world supplies.

11. To instruments the great their glory owe;
The lofty are supported by the low;
  Without assistance rank and skill were vain:

Too oft we spurn the object we should prize ;
The rice denuded unproductive dies,
The husk we scorn preserves the living grain.

12. In bulk the scentless *taly** far excels ;
The little *magul* flower more sweetly smells :
In seeming meanness may be hidden worth :
The spacious sea, with all its vauntful roar,
E'en for ablution fits not,† while ashore
The humble spring with nectar gushes forth.

13. The branching trees that in the jungle grow
No excellence like cultured palms can show :
Appearing proudly with the learned, he
Who, lacking skill to scan the proffer'd verse,
Or seize the sense of what the rest rehearse,
Is disconcerted, stands a jungle tree.

14. As when the clumsy turkey, having seen
The forest peacock step with graceful mien,
Struck with the beauty of his gorgeous train,
And thinking one of kindred plume he spied,
His feathers spread with pomp of strutting pride,
Poetic skill unlearned coxcombs feign.

* A coarse wild flower.

† The saline deposit spoils the look of the brown skin. English blue-jackets sometimes drive canoes away, and make room for their own boat, by naughtily dipping a hand in the sea, and dashing some water on the shoulders of the native sailors.

15. Who aid the ingrate in their yearning zeal,
Like him who dared the poison'd tiger heal,
But raise the prostrate to become their prey ;
And, like the vase that greets the granite block,
Or freighted bark that strikes the sunken rock,
Their blind beneficence is thrown away.

16. The noble in distress are still esteem'd ;
The mean of wealth bereft are worthless deem'd ;
The former like a cup of gold are found
That, fractured, its intrinsic worth retains ;
The latter like an earthen bowl, that gains
Contempt when strew'd in fragments on the ground.

17. Insult not over those in self-conceit
Whose self-restraint may end in your defeat,
Though void they seem of wisdom, tact, and strength :
If smaller fish may dart securely by,
The heron watches with unerring eye
The proper victim, that appears at length.

18. No friends are they who heartlessly forsake,
As water-fowl the sun-exhausted lake,
Their old associates in their time of need :
As lilies wither when the pond gets dry,
And, where they flourish'd, parch'd and prostrate lie,
Who share our troubles are our friends indeed.

19. Say, fretful spirit, whether shall ensue
The visionary good we fondly view,
Or every just award decreed by fate?
From Indra's tree, for fruits of blessing known,
Who gilded nuts of poison pluck, atone
For deeds that stain'd their pre-existent state.

20. Because in ocean dipp'd, not four times more
The measure holds than it could hold before.
What futile hopes our silly sex employ!
Though wealth be gain'd, and spousal sweets abound,
No greater happiness is therefore found,
Since fate has fix'd the limits of our joy.

21. 'Tis not in blood that kindred only lies,
From birth connections that true friendships rise;
Disease congenital may mortal prove:
As distant mountains may the med'cine yield
By which alone a sickness can be heal'd,
A stranger may desponding care remove.

22. The dwelling with a frugal mistress bless'd,
Though all things lacking, is of all possess'd,
For peace, content, and cleanliness are there;
The house not suited with a thrifty wife,
Or cursed with one intent on angry strife,
Though plenty reign, is like the tiger's lair.

23. The learned to the erudite repair,
As seeks the swan the placid water, where
The lotus breathes its genial fragrance round;

But like the crow, by carrion-instinct led,
That scents the grave and lives upon the dead,
The ignorant are with the foolish found.

24. By hasty wrath disjoin'd, the meaner kind,
Like broken stone, are never more combined;
Remingle soon the better sort their hearts,
Like fractured gold by fusion blent again;
No longer sunder'd do the best remain
Than water that the pointed arrow parts.

25. While, conscious of his fatal power to harm,
The guilty cobra hides in just alarm,
The guileless water-snake abroad appears:
Deceivers so, avoiding public view,
In secret their perfidious schemes renew,
While innocence at large no danger fears.

26. Though servile hosts the king's behests obey,
The grave philosopher bears ampler sway;
While homage meets the sage wherever known,
And every step extends his spotless fame,
The monarch's title is an empty name
Beyond the narrow realms that prop his throne.

27. To fools, the words of the resentful wise,
To vicious souls, the virtue they despise,
As plantains to the stalk from which they sprung,*

* Having yielded one bunch of fruit, the trunk of the banana or plantain-tree perishes, making room for the virgin stalks springing from its root. In gardens, the old stem, having served its turn, is immediately cut down.

Are terrible as Yama's * fatal name ;
But better still this suits the tyrant dame,
  They know, who fear and feel her clam'rous
    tongue.

28. Attrition, in its merciless delay,
May wear the precious sandal-wood away,
  But leaves its grateful fragrance all behind :
So, though calamities their coffers drain,
Triumphant o'er misfortune, kings retain
  Their royal fortitude of heart and mind.

29. With Lakshmi come, and vanish when she flies,
The pleasures that from constant friendships rise,
  Resources keeping pace with high desire,
The pride of beauty, dignity of birth,
And all things loved and coveted on earth ;
  Then, toil for wealth, and prize what you
    acquire.

30. Till by the ringing axe in ruin laid,
As trees afford a cool refreshing shade
  To mortals shrinking from the scorching heat,
The sons of knowledge, till they cease to live,
As far as can be, good for evil give,
  And acts of kindness to their foes repeat.

* Death.

ATTISUDI.

The chance of doing good desire.
Extinguish anger's kindling fire.
The means at your command confess.
Be no one hinder'd who would bless.
Of riches do not idly brag.
Let zeal and courage never flag.
Letters and numbers claim esteem.
All shameless begging shameful deem.
Give alms, then eat with gratitude.
Be customs gratefully pursued.
No idle pause in learning seek.
A word of envy never speak.
Make not the price of corn to rise.
Let candid lips report your eyes.
Consort, like letters in array.
The day to bathe is Saturday.*

* In this weekly ceremony, the head is first smeared with oil and other substances, and water is afterwards affused. The rule for it is thus given in a Tamil stanza :—"If you bathe on Sunday, death will seize you ; if on Monday, you cannot gain the favour of God; if on Tuesday," the day assigned to the widow, "you will fall sick ; if on Thursday, sorrow will oppress you ; if on holy Friday," so called because a day kept as sacred to Lakshmi and Parvati by many women, "you will lose your property : avoid all these, and anointing bathe on Wednesday and Saturday." Saturday is a somewhat sacred day. A worshipper of Vishnu

Your speech with pleasant words be fill'd.
Do not too large a dwelling build.
When friends you find, be found a friend.
With fond regard your parents tend.
Remember every kindly deed.
In seed-time sow the precious seed.
Don't wrest and eat another's ground.
Be all your practice comely found.
Who sport with snakes, with danger jest.
Upon a bed of cotton rest.
Disdain to breathe a word of guile.
No graceless deeds your name defile.
Let learning be in youth your choice.
Remember virtue's form and voice.
In early morn, drive sleep away.
Say nothing cruel all the day.
To fasting due attention give.
By proper living, teach to live.
For baseness give no cause to chide.
Good tempers never lay aside.
United with your friend remain.
Avoid inflicting wrong or pain.
They learn the most, the most who try.
Your trade be free to own and ply.

expressed to the writer his regret that Christians had so declined that, in the face of their own *shastras*, they had ceased to observe the seventh day as the day of rest and worship. But for this change, he remarked, they would have had common ground on which to stand with seriously disposed Hindus.

Nor steal, nor wish to take away.
Refrain from every sinful play.
In ways of justice keep your feet.
Be found where saints and sages meet.
In speech be open and sincere.
To what is excellent adhere.
Nothing provoking anger say.
With gamesters have no wish to play.
In all you do, correctness show.
Go where you know you ought to go.
Your steps from fault-detecting stay.
Say plainly what you have to say.
Get not the wand'ring idler's name.
Acquire the well-known worthy's fame.
Let priests your cheerful presents view.
To Perumal * pay service due.
From sin desist, and evil chase.
To care and trouble give no place.
Consider well ere you essay.
Despise not God, but keep His way.
Live with your countrymen agreed.
The words of women do not heed.
The things of eld be kept in view.
No doubtful, dangerous course pursue.
Hold fast the good until the end.
Perform such acts as all commend.
Where you were born, contented stay.

* Vishnu.

You should not in the water play.
Be dainties from your table spurn'd.
Let many sciences be learn'd.
The rice-field diligently tend.
Be righteousness your way and end.
From fatal evils stand afar.
With no low words your language mar.
By no excess disease induce.
Bespatter none with foul abuse.
Contract no friendship with a snake.
With wicked lips no mischief make.
By patient toil at greatness aim.
In all your living, live for fame.
First till the ground, then eat your rice.
Consult your betters for advice.
Let ignorance be put away.
With children neither join nor stay.
Retain what you possess, and thrive.
Nor stir to angry strife, nor strive.
Preserve your mind from trouble free.
Yield nothing to an enemy.
Your words be but the few you need.
Do not immoderately feed.
From where contention rages run.
Perverse and stupid people shun.
Only at home caresses seek.
Incline the ear when wise men speak.
Avoid the doors where harlots dwell.
Correctly told be all you tell.

Throw every sinful lust aside.
Boast not your parts with foolish pride.
In strife be not your word the first.
In knowledge covet to be versed.
Be heaven your first and final aim.
Acquire the good man's fragrant name.
Live happily among your own.
Be sharp in neither word nor tone.
Desiring, do not therefore stray.
Awake and rise at break of day.
All intercourse with foes refuse.
Say nothing based on partial views.

CONDAY-VĒNTHAN.

Our parents first of all the gods are known.
  From temple worship matchless good accrues.
True virtue lives in married life alone.
  What niggards heap the wicked get and use.
In little eating female beauty lies.
  His country's foe both branch and root decays.
Figures and letters are a pair of eyes.
  Our children's balm-like fondness age delays.
Your duty do, though with a beggar's fare.
  One master serving, in one district stay.
Good life in priests surpasses sounding prayer.
  The slanderer's substance quickly melts away.
In seeking land and treasure spend your days.
  The wife who heeds her lord's commands is chaste.
In being watch'd consists the sex's praise.*
  Objects of vain pursuit, forget with haste.
Speak modestly, though by inferiors heard.
  The man who looks at faults no kindred own.
Though sharp your arrow, use no braggart word.
  All hurtful things are better let alone.

* Not so says the *Cural*, vi. 57.

The firm once ruin'd substance repossess.
  The rich are poor when wisdom's wealth appears.
The monarch's smile brings succour to distress.
  Slander is wind to fire in willing ears.
The heartless railer all men hate and shun.
  No loving children bless the debauchee.
The pride of parents is a learned son.
  True penance theirs, engross'd who Siva see.
In husbandry is trod the path of gain.
  The worth of kindred is their being nigh.
Gambling and brawling lead to grief and pain.
  Forgotten penance makes good fortune fly.
Till midnight sleep not, though confined and still.
  Before you dine, give alms, however small.
Of good and joy the rich can have their fill.
  To vagrant beggary the idle fall.
No word excels a father's sage decree.
  If not a mother's, no advice is wise.
In search of wealth, e'en cross the fearful sea.
  From quenchless anger endless quarrels rise.
A stubborn wife's a firebrand in the breast.
  She's death who gives the winds your faults to show.
God's wrath aroused, in vain men do their best.
  Who spend, yet nothing get, to ruin go.
Beneath a roof in *Tay* and *Masi* * sleep.
  The freeman's plough procures the sweetest food.
From friends themselves your want a secret keep.
  Who lack good company, in sorrow brood.

* January and February, the dewy season.

No ills invade a neighbour-loving land.
  By every word you calmly speak abide.
Your dwelling fix where wells are at command.
  The smallest matters thoughtfully decide.
The laws you know consistently observe.
  No mask to others hides from self one's mind.
They fast in vain, from rules who idly swerve.
  Though poor your hearer, let your speech be kind.
By diligence the mean may mighty grow.
  He does not fast who hungrily devours.
The springing blades the coming crop foreshow.
  Take food, though rice and milk, at proper hours.
'Tis virtue from another's home to stay.
  Reserve your equal strength the load to bear.
Eat not of flesh, nor steal, nor dare to slay.
  The base the garb of virtue cannot wear.
Who gain the highest state, nor hate nor love.
  Simplicity is woman's jewel bright.
The earth bears longest those who gently move.
  All kinds of evil banish out of sight.
The ploughman's honest meal is food indeed.
  With guests your meat, however costly, share.
Where rain is wanted, there is every need.
  The welcome showers succeed the lightning's glare.
The ship without a pilot makes no head.
  At eve, the fruit of morning's acts you reap.
There's nectar found in what the ancients said.
  Who softly lie, enjoy the sweetest sleep.

What wealth the plough produces will remain.
  In silence wisdom has its end and proof.
Their efforts, who disdain advice, are vain.
  From black-eyed women go, and keep aloof.*
Be all excess e'en by the king eschew'd.
  No showers descending, fee-less Brahmans smart.
Good manners hospitality include.
  A hero's friendship pierces like a dart.
The poor who scorn to beg deserve respect.
  The strength of wealth in perseverance lies.
The incorrupt deceitful thoughts reject.
  Let but the king be angry, succour flies.
Go, worship God in every fane on earth.
  Choose places fit wherein to close your eyes.
The lagging student gains nor lore nor worth.

* Courtesans blacken their eyelids.

GARLAND OF ADVICE FOR WOMEN.

Hear advice, my lass, and heed it.
Share your rice with those who need it.
Find no joy in others' sadness.
Live to give your parents gladness.
Let not guile within you labour.
Earn the praise of every neighbour.
Why should anything distress you ?
Give the needy cause to bless you.
Tortoise-like, restrain the senses.
Virtue gives a house pretences.
Beauty's woman's wealth, not science.
Ouvvay's precepts claim compliance.
Shine in every household duty.
Tending well is wifehood's beauty.
Worship your good man each morning.
Shrink from fraud, though poor, with scorning.
Fame with pleasant words be gaining.
Gentle dames are uncomplaining.
Bickering suits not loyal spouses.
Err not, entering others' houses.
When you ask for counsel, take it.
Owning aught, your husband's make it.
Flowers in tufted hair are pleasing.
Cow-like shame at home is teasing.

Ribald words are seemly never.
What 's a head-wife, if not clever?
Telling lies is sure to hurt you.
Sweet is firm domestic virtue.
Void of virtue, earth were charmless.
Who will blame you, if you 're harmless.
Game and strife misfortunes gender.
Right to all impartial render.
Friends, when true, are never distant.
Talk by gesture 's inconsistent.
Do as Wisdom's lips advise you.
Go astray, and all despise you.
Brag not, bravely self-reliant.
Let your master find you pliant.
Water to the parch'd deny not.
Slumbering after sun-rise lie not.
Sin is virtue's paths not keeping.
Let not mid-day see you sleeping.
Satan-like 's * calumniating.
Think of God when meditating.
Wasting's losing all your getting.
Why should women e'er be fretting?
Food enough provide, and spread it.
Be your caste's delight and credit.
Mark your mother's steps, pursuing.
Hell 's not purchased by well-doing.
By your husband's words be guided.
Truth who speak, are not derided.

* Cuttu-like. Cuttu is a name of Yama.

Never Nili's * name inherit.
All you hear 's not void of merit.
Boast not, though you have a hundred.
Falseness from your heart be sunder'd.
Virtue 'll ever be befriended.
Store no malice when offended.
Haughty dark words be unspoken.
Fasts must not too soon be broken.
Roe-like leaping brings repenting.
Hunger's face behold, relenting.
Bad's the fruit of sinful walking.
Children cure of evil talking.
Health is cleanly, wash your linen.
Praises virtue's sure of winning.
Flower-like live, a fragrant treasure.
From the sex come power and pleasure.
Artless women wear the graces.
Softly move with order'd paces.
Early bathe you, saffron using.
Loving strife is credit losing.
Honest matrons awe the ocean.
Glory crowns a wife's devotion.
Reverence your husband's mother.
Proud provoking tempers smother.
Fish-eyed looks at strangers take not.
Sullen nasal murmurs make not.

* A name of Cali. Hence a common name for a malicious woman.

Workers have no sleeping corner.
Gentle lips provoke no scorner.
Aim on earth at praises winning.
Madly seek not joy in sinning.
Nothing say to your undoing.
Fraudful deeds are fraught with ruin.
Teeth like jasmin-buds display you.
Valluvar's wife's pattern sway you.
Look for evil if you quarrel.
Though in sport, say nought immoral.
Set the lamp, ere dark your dwelling.
Aim in cooking at excelling.
Helping neighbours, help them truly.
Clean the house each Friday duly.
Fast by Scripture regulation.
Gain the country's commendation.
Willing walk above correction.
Proverbs point you to perfection.
In the way of good progressing,
Get and gain by every blessing.

Memorials of Cabilar, etc.

THE second son of Pagavan and Athy was born and left in a rest-house at Tiruvārūr (Trivalore), in the cloud-blessed Chōla country. Pāppayan, a Brahman of the place, whose grief was that he had no child, walking in that direction, saw the pretty babe, and was as delighted as a poor man would be on finding in a lonely spot a vessel of gold. He gently took up the stranger, and carried it home; and his wife received it kindly. In the face of the world, Pāppayan named the boy CABILAR, and brought him up as his own son. He grew in wisdom, and was remarkable for good conduct. When he had reached the age of seven, the time for investment with the sacred cord, all the Brahmans in the town were invited to join in the appropriate ceremonies. They met accordingly, but with one voice refused to assist, on the ground that the candidate was not born in their caste. Pāppayan was overwhelmed with disappointment; but his lamentations were soon interrupted. The boy himself, divinely favoured, appeared in the assembly, and maintained his right, composing and chanting the following poem. "It is nothing," he argued, "to say that caste comes by birth: it is won by deeds." Unable to gainsay his remonstrance, the wondering Brahmans now, with as much delight as his foster-parents, initiated him into the privileges of their order. Strange that, in spite of this popular history, caste has obtained so strong a hold in India! The poet Pattira-Kiriyār asks,—"O when will the time come that men shall live together without any distinction of caste, according to the doctrine promulgated in the beginning by Cabilar?"

He had already gained a seat as one of the forty-nine professors in the Madura College, when Tiru-Valluvar presented his *Cural* for approval; and he gave his judgment in the following stanza:—

"The *Cural*, of fair lands O king,
Where tutor'd birds in houses sing,
Till lull'd by women's sweeter song,
Though short in words, in sense is long,
On millet blade as dew-drop small
Reflected shows the palm-tree tall."

It may be interesting here to say what is written of the other four wonderful foundlings. Ouvvay was the eldest, Cabilar the fifth, and Valluvar the youngest of the children.

UPPAY, the second, born in a choultry at Ūttu-Cadu, a place of fountains, as the name indicates, was taken possession of by a washerman, became a distinguished poetess, wrote a treatise on ethics, and after death was deified under the title of Mariyammay.

ATHIGAMĀN, the eldest son and third child, abandoned in a grove at Caruvūr, was brought up by a king of the Chēra country, became an accomplished archer, grew learned in the wisdom of Menu, and rose to rank and affluence. He was a bountiful patron of bards, and in his mellifluous writings, as all accomplished Tamils testify, presented to the world "the nectar of the poets."

URUVAY, the fourth child, saw the light in a shed at Cāveripatnam, and was taken and reared by a family of Sanars, toddy-dealers. She became a distinguished dancer and poetess, and is now worshipped as a goddess of mischief at Tiruvālangādu.

VALLY, the sixth child, born on the slope of Mount Vēl, was found and adopted by basket-makers. Nothing is on record to her credit.

CABILAR-AGAVAL.*

Of the world, Nanmuga's † grand creation,
With its secret laws, an explanation,
  And its glories, who can render?
O ye sages, did the male sex first,
Or the female, into being burst,
  Or things of the neuter gender?

Does the day or star precedence claim?
From the other which derived its name?
  Which is older, good or ill?
Which must higher, wealth or lore, be rated?
Was the spacious ancient earth created?
  Or a work that knew no will?

Are the births and castes you fondly own
The event of nature's growth alone,
  Or a scheme design'd and finish'd?
Who will live till fate shall fairly call?
Who will prematurely victims fall,
  Their appointed time diminish'd?

* The word *Agaval* is descriptive of the metre of the Tamil poem.

† The Four-faced, *i.e.*, Brahma.

Will infectious evil ever die?
Why and where do all the senses fly,
  When the man that own'd them 's dead?
Do ascetics some new form obtain,
Or acquire a human birth again?
  Is the soul or body fed?

With a ready mouth and tongue I come,
As a drum-stick this, and that a drum:
  Ye good people all attend.
But a hundred years our life can number;
And of these we fifty lose in slumber,
  And in childhood five expend.

Then of thrice five more by youth bereft,
From the hundred we've but thirty left:
  And now joy, now grief, is rife.
What is wealth? a river overflowing.
What is youth? its crumbling bank. And growing
  Like a tree thereon, is life.

So of only one pursuit be heedful;
And from doing well, the one thing needful,
  Not a moment dare to borrow.
This first concern demands to-day,
Nor admits another hour's delay:
  Ye are fools who claim to-morrow.

For you cannot tell what luck is near,
If to-morrow Yama may appear,
  Or another day you'll gain.

Every moment Cuttuvan * expect,
When he comes all worship who'll reject,
And your richest gifts disdain.

You may argue, but you'll be denied;
With your kin he'll not be satisfied;
All alike in death must share:
He will neither from the good man turn,
Nor the needy, nor the wicked spurn,
Nor the man of money spare.

Not a moment will the Fierce-eyed stay;
And the body he 'll not bear away,
With the soul alone content.
For a spirit fled, O men bereaved,
Or a carcase dead, are ye so grieved?
Or for what do you lament?

Do you say ye mourn the spirit's flight?
As it ne'er before appear'd in sight,
So to-day it is not seen.
Do you say the body stirs your grief,
While you watch it still, though like a thief,
When itself has rifled been.

For you strip it; hands and feet you tie;
From the kindred pile the flame mounts high;
Only ashes now remain.

* Yama, Death.

You have laved, and to your kindred go :
Does complacence or regret o'erflow,
  That you mingle tears again?,

With repeated mantras and good cheer,
Will your children keep you lingering here,
  O ye Brahmans, when you die?
To return were suppliant ghosts e'er known,
And with hands outstretch'd keen hunger own,
  And their cravings satisfy?

While the Hunas, Ottyas, Singhalese,
And the Mlechas, Yavanas, Chinese,
  And the Chonakas,* and others,
Have no Brahmans throughout all their borders,
You have ranged in four exclusive orders
  Whom creation meant for brothers.

It is conduct marks the high and low.
The consorted cow and buffalo
  Were a wonder to be seen.
Do your castes thus mutually repel?
Is their union so impossible?
  Has it never fruitful been?

* The Chinese and Singhalese excepted, these names are now used to signify Mohammedans, infidels, and barbarians. It seems impossible to determine exactly their ancient application. Probably the Arabians were called Chonakas: the Greeks were Yavanas. The other tribes mentioned occupied countries bordering on Hindustan.

Wheresoe'er whatever seed is sown,
It will there produce its kind alone.
  Let a Brahman's progeny,
Though a Puliah * mother gives them birth,
Be accepted by the lords of earth †
  As their equals in degree.

As the cow and buffalo between,
Who have ever such a difference seen
  Among men of divers classes?
In the life men lead, the limbs they wear,
In their bodies, in their form and air,
  And in mind, no rank surpasses.

When a Puliah with a Brahman's mouth
For the north forsakes his native south,
  He is there a Brahman deem'd:
When a Brahman from the north betrays
In the south a Puliah's crooked ways,
  But a Puliah he's esteem'd.

In the mire as crimson lilies grow,
So Vasishta,‡ Brahma's son, we owe
  To a lowly concubine.
A Chandāly § to Vasishta gave
Sattyanāda, by a Puliah slave
  Who prolong'd the famous line.

* Pariah, low-caste. The ancestors of the Puliahs are said to have been circumcised slaves of the Mohammedans.

† Brahmans. Cabilar here describes his own case.

‡ One of the seven great sages, son of the mind of Brahma.

§ A Pariah woman, an outcast.

To Parāsara her son, the birth
Of Vyāsa * seal'd a fish-girl's worth.
  And because all basely born,—
In the Vēdas versed, for learning famed,—
With the very first of sages named,—
  Are they aught of glory shorn?

I am Cabilar, whom Āthy bore
Unto Pagavan in Caruvore,—
  She a Puliah, he the sage;
And I'll tell you how we all have fared,—
For by seven of us is proudly shared
  The unequal parentage.

In a place where ready springs abound,
With a lowly washer, Uppay found
  All the fostering care she needed.
Nor could Uruvay of aught complạin,
Though its juice they from the palm-tree drain
  Who her wants have kindly heeded.

With musicians Ouvvay found a home.
On the mountain side, with those who roam
  In the woods, was Vally bred.
Among Pariahs Valluvar appear'd.
In a grove Athigamān was rear'd,
  Where the bees on flowers fed.

* Compiler of the Vēdas.

Gentle Brahmans I am bound to bless
Who these richly-water'd lands possess,
For their never-failing care.
Does the rain keep clear of men low-born?
Do the breezes in their progress scorn?
Does the earth disdain to bear?

Does the sun refuse them light and heat?
Does the jungle yield what mean men eat,
While the fields support the high?
All alike may wealth or want inherit;
All alike may earn devotion's merit;
And we all alike must die.

There is but one race o'er all the earth;
Men are one in death, and one in birth;
And the God they serve is One.
Who the sayings of old time revere,
And in virtue firmly persevere,
Are inferior to none.

Who relieve the suppliant day by day,
Who abhor to lie or steal or slay,
Who the fleshly fire subdue,
And who blandly speak, contemn your scorn.
O ye fools, let graces rank adorn,
Or no good does thence accrue.

The Unerring Judge.

THE English found India a continent of political volcanoes, earthquakes, and storms. Caprice and vice ruled in every region. The tyranny of one district was unlike that of another. In the same petty kingdom the succession of a Rajah was a violent introduction of new measures. Iniquity was religion, and morality a dream. The criminal was as often on the bench as in the dock. A bribe was necessary to open the judge's eyes; and he used torture to bring accused persons to his own way of thinking. Prosecutors were liars, and witnesses actors. There was often no standard of law. If a man had property, his head sat loose on his shoulders. Jewels were not safe, even when buried underground. There were treatises on short and easy methods of burglary and slaughter.

We have changed all that, or nearly so. By nothing has India been more benefitted than our impartial administration of justice. The high do not now trample upon the low; and the rights of rich and poor are equally sacred. Venality is a crime, as well as perjury; and the wretch who dares to employ torture is as guilty as the worst criminal to whom it can be applied. Not particular districts only are brightened and healed : the blessing is diffused like the sunshine, and pervasive as the air. The land that was all in pieces has been joined together.

Ere England's power was felt, proof often occurred that "there is a spirit in man, and the inspiration of the Almighty giveth them understanding." As the rainbow paints the cloud, and as stars shine in the night, now and then a genius arose among the natives, whose face shone with God's image, and in whose hands were the tables of His law. Reason, conscience, and common sense spread their gifts in his proceedings ; and there was refuge and protection for the people till the lofty tree was laid low. "For they saw that the wisdom of God was in him, to do judgment." When he fell, it was like the withdrawal of Divine favour ; and the exposed country sighed and smarted.

The following Tamil history gives a glimpse of such a hero. It is a specimen of the tales current at this day among our eastern fellow-subjects, being, with the exception that a story unfit for our language has been omitted, a faithful translation of one out of many such works issued from the native press. A few connecting words only have been added ; and, as far as possible, the indelicate expressions characteristic of Hindu publications have been rejected. Not free from fiction, yet it is most likely founded upon fact.

The narrative exemplifies the old despotic practice of elevating men, with no special training, and on the impulse of an hour, to the highest offices. One day RĀMAN had the applause of children with whom he played: the next he was the man whom the king delighted to honour. This record of cases in which he is said to have given judgment shows how serviceable to a shrewd magistrate is circumstantial evidence; and it exhibits the disposition of the Hindu to cheat and lie, and his opinion that falsehood is pardonable if only clever.

The wisdom of the East speaks in proverbs. When any striking event is witnessed or related, it is usual to quote as the moral of it some common saying. It will be observed that each of the following stories illustrates a popular adage cited at its close.

Our hero belonged to the Velāla or agriculturist caste, one of the most respectable, and was a native of Chōla-Mandalam, or, as modern geography has it, Coromandel. The meaning of the word is, *The Country of Chōla*, spoken of in previous pages; and the present name shows where that good land lay. Its ancient capital was Urayūr; but the kings more recently resided at Tanjore. Their dynastic appellation was *Chōlan;* and a proud title it was. By cutting canals from the river Cāvery, those monarchs made their territory the most fertile in India. Eastern exaggeration says, not that it was a land flowing with milk and honey, but that ghee was to be drawn from a reservoir in its metropolis like water from a well.

The rulers prided themselves on their justice. A

common saying in India for governing so that no one shall have cause to complain is, "governing so that not even the tongue of the bell shall move." This saying originated in the use made of the familiar instrument by a Chōla king. He had a bell hung up at his palace-gate, that by means of it such as failed to obtain redress from his subordinates might attract his royal notice. Alas! even in happy Chōla the tongue was not always still. Our history introduces itself with a case in which a woman who had been imposed upon, if she did not ring the bell, wrung her hands, and, instead of His Majesty's clapper, made good use of her own.

The judgments of Rāman will remind the reader of the famous decision of Solomon,* and of similar stratagems adopted in cases of litigation by Claudius, Ariopharnes, and others mentioned by commentators. There are still transitional countries, fallen from civilization, or not risen to it, in which justice is administered according to the law of a judge's sagacity or a ruler's ready wit. An apposite anecdote of the Bey of Tunis occurs in a recent publication.

" A certain Moor lost his purse one day, containing sundry gold pieces or sequins. Desirous of recovering it, he proclaimed his mishap by means of the good offices of the town-crier. The person who had found it was an upright man, conspicuous for his probity; and the moment he discovered to whom it belonged,

* 1 Kings iii. 16—28.

he made haste to restore it to its rightful owner: but the latter, finding that he had to do with a rich man, thought it a good opportunity for a little illicit gain at the expense of him who had so conscientiously restored it. He therefore maintained that there were eighty sequins missing out of the purse in question, and violently insisted on their restitution. The quarrel became uproarious, and of course was referred to the decision of the Bey. One man declared that the purse originally contained a hundred sequins, whilst his adversary affirmed with many oaths that he had given it back just as he found it. As both assertions bore the same aspect of probability, the Bey was for a moment embarrassed as to his decision. He asked however, to see the purse, and having examined it attentively, withdrew from it the money it contained, ordering, at the same time, that another hundred sequins be brought from his own treasury. He tried to put them into the purse, which, however, would only contain about fifty; then emptying it afresh, he invited the prosecutor to try his hand at it, and fill it with the hundred sequins which he had sworn it originally to enclose. Of course he was unable to do so; and the Bey, handing the purse and the sequins to the defendant, said, 'You had better take possession of it, as it does not answer the description given of it.' The false accuser received two hundred blows from the bastinado." *

* "Under the Palms in Algeria and Tunis." By the Hon. Lewis Wingfield. 1868.

MARIYATHAY-RĀMAN.

I.

ONE OF FOUR THIEVES
THE REST DECEIVES.

Four lodgers with an ancient dame
Received contentedly what came,
Were gainers by what others lost,
And boarded at the public cost.
Now coins and jewels music yield,
Within a brazen vessel seal'd;
But they must keep the common prey
To charm them on a safer day.
" Ho, bury this beneath the floor,
Till call'd for, mother, by all four,"
They said, and still their lodgings kept,
And ate and drank, and watch'd and slept.
Once on a day, as o'er the way
In a verandah's shade they lay,
And of the common good conversed,
The faithful four were plagued with thirst.
"Who'll go to the old dame, and say
That we must have a pot of whey?" *

* Buttermilk, esteemed none the worse for being sour, is a favourite drink in India for quenching thirst. It is usual to take

Was ask'd; and, flying like a shot,
One said to her, "Produce the pot."
Pledged not to part with it at all
Without an order from them all,
Into the street she trusty went,
And ask'd if for the pot they'd sent.
"Yes, give it him, and don't be slow."
So, turning back, an iron crow
She lent her lodger, and reveal'd
The place where she'd the jar conceal'd.
"With this you'll turn it up with ease,"
Said she; and he was on his knees.
The metal in his hands he feels,
And then the mettle in his heels;
Through the back door he bears the prize;
And like a thief of thieves he flies.
  Minutes twice twelve the thirsty three
Had waited, wondering not to see
Their partner with a pot supplied,
When all got up, and went inside.

it early in the morning; and no doubt the dry souls had passed a feverish night. With the exception of the messenger, they had now allowed their wits to go to sleep. The direction they gave him,—*Tondi yeduttuk kondu va*,—was ambiguous; one of its words, *tondi*, being either a verbal participle or a noun. The noun means *a small earthen vessel;* the participle, *having dug in the ground*. The words therefore not only signify, "Bring a small jar," but equally, "Dig up, and bring." The intended meaning was evident from the addition, "to get some whey;" but that addition the rogue suppressed, it not being true always that there is honour among thieves.

The cheat perceived, the dame they cursed ;
And vengeance now was all their thirst.
They hail'd her to the judgment-bar,
And swore she 'd stolen their brazen jar.
The Lord Chief Justice weigh'd the case,
Look'd the poor woman in the face,
And said he could not let it pass,
She must restore the pot of brass.
" O dear ! what shall I do ? " she cries,
And tears are streaming from her eyes.
As bright a youth as e'er you'll meet
Was in the middle of the street,
With playmates busy at the game
Of pitch and toss : * he ask'd the dame,
" Good grandmother, why all these tears ? "
She with her story fill'd his ears.
Then, turning to his play anew,
As from his hands the nuts he threw,
Exclaim'd the grieved precocious soul,
" May these as surely find the hole
As earth his mouth shall quickly choke
Who this unrighteous sentence spoke ! " †

* *Ketcheyk-kay*, something like a game of marbles ; instead of marbles, areka nuts being used. The aim in it is, from a fixed distance, to pitch the nuts into one or more of two or three holes scooped in the ground.

† The allusion is to the situation of a buried corpse, uncoffined, with the face turned up ; and the wish conveyed the opinion that the gods would not allow so unrighteous a judge to live very long. The prophecy of the youth was fulfilled. The mouth of

Some busybodies to the throne
Made Rāman's daring comment known.
The boy was to the monarch led,
And thus the awful Chōlan said,
"Who thinks the sentence so unjust,
Himself the case may try, and must."
The child of Menu, unappall'd,
The prisoner and the plaintiffs call'd,
The matter sifted, set her free,
And thus address'd the baffled three:
"She will, as pledged, the jar restore,
When told to do so by all four."
Grief goes the way that treasures go,*
They say: the lady found it so.
The king with joy the tidings heard,
The title of "The Just" † conferr'd
On Rāman, made the bench his own,
Sent gifts of honour from the throne,
With special countenance caress'd,
And held him a familiar guest.

the unfortunate gentleman was filled with dirt: he was as good as dead.

* 1. Wealth in possession is grief, in the anxiety it occasions. This grief ceases when the wealth disappears. 2. When property is stolen, the greater affliction is with the stealer. The unfortunate loser is less unhappy than the miserable thief.

† *Mariyathay*, The Unerring.

II.

How one denied Infanticide.

When made aware of what was done,
The father, trembling for his son,
And for himself, with anger said,
" O Rāman, have you lost your head?
By subtilties of justice vex'd,
The very gods are oft perplex'd;
And who to master them are you?
From one mistake will scores ensue.
This office full of fear decline,
And show not where you cannot shine."
Rāman the Just made answer, " Sire,
There's small occasion for your ire;
Since God will be my faultless Guide,
And aid me wisely to decide.
Pray do not force me to refuse,
But let the king my station choose;
Nor fortune's goddess kick away,
When she a visit deigns to pay."
"Do as you like," he then replied,
Unable to say aught beside,
And home again his footsteps bent,
Reflecting as he thither went,
"If here I stay,—more than I dare,—
His slips and troubles I must share.

Attempting, he but tempts, the law.
To other lands I must withdraw." *
His purpose hidden from his son,
Forthwith his journey was begun.
Night reach'd, he at a dwelling lay,
Whose lord had gone from home that day,
Leaving his wives,—the childless first,
And second † who an infant nursed.
The elder woman went to rest.
No slumber sooth'd the quiet guest
Who on the seat outside the door
Lay turning his misfortunes o'er.
Now thinking both in slumber sound,
And that her wish'd-for chance was found,
The second wife at midnight made
The signal her gallant obey'd.
The startled infant at her side
Inopportunely woke, and cried.
Exposure dreading more than death,
She grasp'd it, to restrain its breath,—
A lasting lesson soon convey'd;
And by the first its body laid.
With night she let her lover go.
With daylight she took up her woe,

* It is not in all instances good to have a friend at court. The highest in the king's favour is the nearest to his frown, and may carry his kindred with him in suddenly falling to the lowest place.

† By license of Hindu law.

Beginning loudly to complain
Her rival had the baby slain.
The village heard, the proofs rehearsed,
The envious murderess fiercely cursed,
And, when the mother sought relief
In Rāman's court, display'd their grief.
  By all he'd chanced to see surprised,
The fugitive soliloquized,
" If right he do in this dispute,
I'll trust my son in any suit."
In studious disguise he dress'd,
And near the seat of justice press'd.
  The new-made Judge, with thoughtful look,
The woman's deposition took ;
Was quick his officers to send
The elder wife to apprehend ;
And, when they'd brought her, ask'd her why
She'd caused the little child to die.
" This hell-deserving sin," said she,
" God knows, was never done by me."
" O base and artful woman ! " cried
The younger wife, and said she lied.
Perplex'd, his lordship would be told
If any did the deed behold.
" My eyes beheld," the accuser cried,
" The deed was seen by none beside."
The judge first turn'd to God his mind,
Then ponder'd how the truth to find.

"In dress befitting callous vice,
You both the court must compass thrice,"
He said. Agreed the younger wife.
"I will not, though it cost my life,"
The other thought; then spoke ashamed,
"I'm willing rather to be blamed
And punish'd in a murderer's place;
O drive me not to this disgrace."
Observing carefully the two,
Rāman the vile dissembler knew,
By stripes constrain'd her to confess,
And hang'd the actual murderess.
The ancient saying was fulfill'd,
"She one thing, God another will'd."
The father then, with boundless joy,
Approach'd and bless'd his wondrous boy.
"Your title and exploit agree:
Rāman the Just my son shall be.
Such wisdom none but God could give.
In health and wealth long may you live!"
And, happy man, he stay'd at home:
What need had he abroad to roam?

III.

Going to law
O'er pussy's paw.

Four partners in the cotton trade,
That rats might not their stores invade,

Procured a cat, and made a law
That each of them should own a paw.
Then each a leg adorn'd with rings
And ankle-chains and beaded strings,
Till, tortured by the glittering load,
A wounded foot grimalkin show'd.*
A strip of cloth the owner found,
And dipp'd in oil, and wrapp'd around.
The kindly embers pussy sought;
The lurking fire the bandage caught;
The flying cat the flame convey'd,
And burnt up all the stock in trade.
  The three, who all the ruin saw,
Resolved to get redress in law;
Their partner before Rāman brought,
And utmost compensation sought.
What they had lost, he should provide
The oily dressing who'd applied.
The judge the claim unrighteous thought:
No wilful damage had been wrought.
He must the prisoner set free,
And turn his sentence on the three.
"The bandaged foot was lame, and so
Could not assist the cat to go:
Its going caused what you lament:
By means of your three legs it went:

* People who kill with kindness, as they do no good, get none.

So you must, be it understood,
To the accused his loss make good."
  They only added to their woes,
As with its own proboscis throws
The elephant, in baffled tread,
The blinding dust upon its head.
The man accused, from lowest grief
In highest joy found quick relief,
Proving, like sailor tempest-toss'd,
Yet 'scaping when confused and lost,
Himself not knowing east from west,
"'Tis God who succours the distress'd." *

IV.

No pearls were e'er Placed in his care!

A man who own'd two pearls of cost,
Determined they should not be lost,
When starting on a journey, thought
He'd leave them in safe hands, and sought
A trusty friend, and saying, "Please,
Till I return, take care of these,"
Contented left his wealth behind,
And travell'd with an easy mind.
  In time, his journey at an end,
He call'd to thank his honest friend,

* Our own proverb is similar :—"Man's extremity is God's opportunity."

Who, to his sore amaze, denied,
"No pearls did you to me confide."
 Forthwith he to the judge complain'd;
And Rāman the accused arraign'd,
And read his guilt upon his face;
But, wanting proof to seal the case,
Heard what each party had to say,
And coolly sent them both away.
 He saw, ere many suns had shone,
The loser of the pearls alone,
And ask'd, with cautious scrutiny,
What sort and size the pearls might be.
Then took he from his casket straight
Of such-like pearls just *ninety-eight*,
And strung them on some rotten thread,
And sent for the accused, and said,
"An honest face like your's I'll trust.
So take these *hundred* pearls you must,
And bring them newly strung; for see,
This cord's as rotten as't can be."
 The joyful rogue went home, and there
The pearls he strung with cunning care,
Then counted them,—again,—again,
And search'd about the floor in vain.
Two pearls he'd lost! so with the rest
He strung the two that he possess'd,
And then, presenting all, proclaim'd
Himself the thief he had been named.

Among the hemp the fowl that dares
To scratch with greed its feet ensnares.
The owner had his pearls return'd,
The thief the punishment he'd earn'd.

V.

THE IRON FED
THE RATS, ONE SAID.

Ten pigs * of iron having bought,
A man a trusty neighbour sought,
And left them in his careful hands,
While he should visit foreign lands.
Some years ere his return transpired,
When for the iron he inquired.
The saucy keeper shook his head,
And, " Rats have eaten it," he said.
Indignantly the owner strode
To Rāman, and his grievance show'd.
The judge upon a measure hit
By which the biter should be bit.
The plaintiff saw the promised fun,
And undertook it should be done ;
In seeming friendship learn'd to smile,
As taught the saw concerning guile,—
" The fondness of a kinsman show,
Your foeman's house to overthrow."

* 10 params = 5,000 lbs.

He fetch'd one day his neighbour's boy
To share a homely feast of joy.
The willing youth the threshhold cross'd,
And in a room was lock'd and lost.
Next morning, when his father cried,
"Where is my child?" the host replied,
"A kite has pounced on him at play,
And borne the screaming boy away."
The parent Rāman's presence sought,
To whom the kidnapper was brought.
The judge demanded, "Can you say
A kite convey'd his son away?"
"I placed," he answered, "in his care
Ten pigs of iron: ask him where
They are, and hear if he'll repeat
That rats did all my iron eat."
The judge severely eyed the twain,
And, frowning, said in angry vein,
"The trick each on the other tries
Is covering a whole gourd with rice.
The father must the iron yield;
The boy no longer be conceal'd."

VI.

NEVER TO ME
LENT SHE THE GHEE.

Two cows a woman kept; but o'er
The way another own'd a score,

Who, midst her plenty, ask'd if she
Would lend her a few pounds of ghee,
And, when the time for payment came,
Denied that she'd received the same.
  The former therefore found the face
Of Rāman, and explain'd the case.
When summon'd, and with questions tried,
The guilty borrower replied,
"I've twenty cows, and she's but two;
'Tis envy makes her falsely sue."
In doubt the judge sent them away,
To come again the following day.
  Ere they arrived, where they must tread,
He had the ground with mire o'erspread.
With muddy feet the women stood
Before him in bewilder'd mood.
His lordship, at their plight appall'd,
For brazen jars of water call'd,
And to the bearers gave command
To each an equal jar to hand.
The poorer woman made her clean,
And yet half-full her jar was seen.
An empty jar the other placed,
Yet half the filth her feet disgraced.
Then could the judge unerring see
Which dairy-dame had wanted ghee.
Her faculty of management
Proved that the poorer one had lent.

The wasteful owner of the score
Was more than sentenced to restore.
The ancient proverb came to mind,—
" The lowest place will water find."

VII.

Give what you choose,
You'll meet my views.

A loving father near his end,
Handed a tried and trusty friend
Ten thousand pagods, that the same
Might be disposed of in his name.
" Give what you like,"—his will so ran,—
" To my dear son when grown a man."
The friend devoted saw him die,
Took home the gold, and put it by.
  When in due time the boy up-grown
Applied to him to have his own,—
" What I should like, your father told,
Must be your portion of the gold.—
Now this is what I like," said he,
And let him but a thousand see.
The youth exclaim'd, " That will not do,"
And angry to the court-house flew.
  The guardian's plea his lordship heard,
And judged him after his own word :—
" The thousands nine you like, 'tis plain,
Since they are what you would retain :

The thousands nine you must let go,
To give him what you like, you know:
What you don't like learn to enjoy,
The tithe you offer'd to the boy."*

Nothing was gain'd by greed of gold,
According to the saying old,
"With demon-swiftness though he fly,
Who'll catch his neighbour's property?"

VIII.

He found it hard,
Who'd robb'd the bard.

A lonely bard, his wandering o'er,
Returning with his gather'd store,
Drew near the town with weary feet,
When it was his mischance to meet
A man who seized his bag, and swore,
"'Tis mine," and home the bundle bore.

* A story for the orator, begging a good collection. Do people give what they like? It is matched by the following anecdote from the Rev. B. Gregory's book, "The Thorough Business Man." "A colleague of the writer's in a London Methodist Circuit had been preaching one Sunday morning on the golden rule, and was dining with a member of the congregation. His host said to him, 'Mr. Hardcastle, I do not quite see your point. You say, Whatsoever ye would that men should do unto you, do ye even so to them. Well, I should very much like you to give me a thousand pounds!' 'O,' replied the minister, 'your duty is perfectly clear: you must please hand *me* a thousand pounds; for, Whatsoever *ye* would, etc.'"

There yet was hope, the poet saw,
While Rāman minister'd the law.
  Inclined to give the bard relief,
He question'd close the summon'd thief,
Who answer'd, with astonish'd face,
"I nothing know about the case."
Then Rāman form'd his careful plan,
And home dismiss'd the perjured man.
  He had not reach'd his house before
Two spies were lurking by the door.
As in he went, his wife's first word,
"How did your business end?" they heard.
"I baffled them, and got scot free,
By feigning ignorance," said he.*
  Their hiding-place the spies forsook,
And their report to Rāman took.
He had the rogue put in arrest.
To scourging all would be confess'd;
As ancient sages truly spoke,
"The grind-stone yields to stroke on stroke."
And when he'd been examined well,
And tortured all his guilt to tell,
And back his bag the bard had gain'd,
He suffer'd as the law ordain'd.

* "Pitchers have ears." It is not safe for the dishonest to open their lips, even in their own dwellings.

IX.

He would not own He held the stone.

One who a sardius possess'd,
To have his anxious mind at rest,
Committed to a merchant's hand
The priceless gem, with this command,—
"I go abroad, some time to stay,—
Take care of this while I'm away."
  Returning when four years had flown,
He ask'd the trader for the stone,
Who said persistently, "You know,
You had it back some time ago."
Than cash more ready with a lie
Three customers for rice stood by,
A washer, black who white could make,
A potter, skill'd the mould to take,
A barber, who could closely shave;
And all would witness for the knave.
They heard his lips the word declare,
And sold themselves the same to swear.
  Observing this, the injured man
To Rāman the Unerring ran,
The stealing of the gem explain'd,
And how false swearers were retain'd.
  The secret whisper'd in his ear,
The judge commanded to appear

The merchant who had done the wrong,
And bring his witnesses along;
And having heard what each could say,
He order'd all the five away.
Confined in silence, each alone
Must shape in clay the precious stone.
With ease the' accuser and the' accused
Fac-similes apart produced;
But vainly every witness tried
To show what he had never eyed.
The barber's gem was like a hone;
The washerman's, a washing-stone;
The potter's, that he deftly holds
When the revolving earth he moulds.
Remarking how these disagreed,
The judge from all his doubts was freed.
The gem its owner repossess'd:
Due punishment o'erwhelm'd the rest.
The flame the pois'nous nightshade earns,
The cotton-tree contiguous burns.
Who sided with the lying thief
Together with him came to grief.

X.

ONE CLAIM'D WITH STRIFE
ANOTHER'S WIFE.

A wife, obedient to a word,
The country tramp'd behind her lord.

Across their path a river ran :
They forded it, he in the van.
A stranger unperceived drew near,
And silent waded in their rear.
Her dress the woman lifted high
Amid the stream, to keep it dry.
The wretch who follow'd her could see
A fish-like mole behind her knee.
The woman was his wife, he swore,
When they had reach'd the further shore,
And let her lawful husband know
She should no longer with him go.
  The men, not settling it alone,
To Rāman made their quarrel known.
The husband said, " My honest spouse
Is his, this lying scoundrel vows."
The rival question'd, stoutly cried,
" She is my wife ; I have not lied."
Then asked the judge, " Which, let me know,
Brings witnesses the truth to show ? "
The traveller said, " In this strange land
We have no witnesses at hand."
Too vile the foulest sin to fear,
The other answer'd, " I've none here ;
But, if I must, I'll give a sign
To prove the modest woman mine :
If female searchers look, they'll find
A fish-like mole her knee behind."

When they reported such the case,
The judge said, looking in her face,
"Which is your husband, on your word?"
She pointed to her lawful lord.
The puzzle to unravel, he
Gave her to female custody,
And sent the claimants both away
In proper charge till break of day.
At dawn he call'd both to his feet,
The executioner to meet,
Whom he commanded, "Be not slow,
For well the criminal you know;
I've told you which affirm'd the lie;
Proceed, and let the villain die." *
The sword was drawn, and, starting, one
Cried, "Do not kill me,—wrong I've done;"
And, trembling, to the court made known
Whence all the fierce dispute had grown.
The happy husband thanks outpour'd
To have his grateful wife restored.
The alien, punish'd for his crime,
Fulfill'd the saying of old time,—
"What can't be borne if any do,
What can't be borne must suffer too."

* See Justice with bandaged eyes, yet holding the balances truly, and wielding the sword with right effect.

XI.

AN EQUAL LOT
SHARE BRUTE AND POT.

The gay procession's drawing near:
The newly-married pair appear.
To the Velālan bridegroom's sire
By Moslem owner lent on hire,
In trappings proud, a yāney * strong
Majestically steps along.
But sudden fate can strength surprise:
The elephant falls down and dies.
Without delay the father ran,
And thus address'd the Mussulman,—
"By God's decree your yāney's dead:
I'll pay, or find one in its stead."
"Neither its price nor substitute,"
He said, "I'll have my living brute."
With this impossible demand
Before the judge he dared to stand.
Wise Rāman the Velālan heard
Relate the facts as they occurr'd,
And said that he was free from blame;
From God the visitation came;
The Moor must take, for what he'd lost,
Another yāney or its cost.

* Elephant.

But nothing could the fool persuade
To hear the just proposal made.
He swore by the Almighty's name,
" I'll have no other, but the same;
Neither its price nor substitute,
Bring me again my living brute."
Troubled the honest borrower stood,
And Rāman sate in thoughtful mood.
At length he said, " You'll both go home,
And both again to-morrow come."
  He then—by secret message brought—
In private the Velālan taught :—
" You need not, as determined, meet
The Moslem at the judgment-seat.
Have your house-door, not fasten'd, mind,
But insecurely closed : behind
Old pāneys * in the entrance pile.
The Moorman shall be caught with guile.
Before me duly he'll appear :
I'll say, 'Your enemy's not here—
Fetch him.' He'll push your door with haste,
And smash the pots behind it placed.
Then let your lamentations flow,
And weeping to your neighbours go ;
' My pāneys old as old can be,
From ancestors come down to me,

* Earthen pots.

This man has broken,' loudly cry;
And in whatever way he try
To' appease your simulated woe,
'I'll have those pāneys,' let him know."
  All happening as the judge foresaw,
Both reach'd again the court of law.
"This man," the self-defender swore,
"Has smash'd my pāneys, made of yore.
I'll have them back, a precious lot,
A priceless heirloom—every pot."
The judge fix'd on the Moor his eye,
And said, "To this what's your reply?"
He answer'd, "Nobody's to blame:
Yāney and pāney fare the same."
How true the saw, in him was shown,
"Wise fools will loose what wealth they own."

XII.

THE CHIT IS TORN,
THE DEBT FORSWORN.

A citizen for money lent
A note of promise did present.
The lender, when some days had flown,
Demanded payment of the loan.
"I shall," the gentleman replied,
"Be on the hill the town outside
To-morrow; bring the note I sign'd,
And all with interest you'll find."

He went: the note the debtor took,
Examined it with searching look,—
A fire with fuel fresh supplied
Was burning ready at his side,—
Then tore, and cast it in the flame,
And said, " Be off, you have no claim."
The merchant sought the judge's face,
And sorrowfully told his case.
The summon'd rogue heard the demand,
" Why did you tear the note of hand ? "
" No note have I destroy'd," said he,
" This fellow nothing lent to me."
Its size the judge inquired aside.
" A span," the creditor replied.
" Say two, when I in public ask,"
Said Rāman, and resumed his task.
Then from the bench, on his return,
He with judicial aspect stern
Inform'd the lender 't must be learnt
How long the bond was that was burnt.
He solemnly a cubit * named.
The citizen aroused, exclaim'd,
" He lies, your lordship, in his throat,
Calling a span a cubit-note ;
If here such glaring lies he'll dare
How many won't he tell elsewhere ? "
" Ah," said the judge, " my clever man,
How could you know it was a span,

* Two spans.

If not by your own fingers penn'd,
And by you given to your friend?"
  Then not alone the perjurer's due,
As law imposed, the' offender knew;
But all for which the note he'd sign'd
With heavy interest resign'd.
He show'd how well the saying fits,
"A man in haste outruns his wits."

XIII.

ONE ORDERS RICE*
A LIME IN SIZE.

To all who'd purchase, young or old,
A Brahmani refreshments sold.
A traveller beforehand paid
His money, and politely said,
"I'm very hungry,—in a trice
Bring me a lime in bulk of rice."

* The word *rice* may apply to a grain or a quantity. A London publican was fined because, when half-a-pint of a beverage was ordered, he supplied only a glassful. Would one be punished if, pocketing the price of a glassful, when modestly asked for a thimbleful, he should take the simpering customer at his word? An English magistrate might not require him even to return the money. Let us appeal to our Indian Solomon. If men were true in speech, to what large mouths they would own! How their requests would expand, if they used words commensurate with their appetites! Would not the dainty sometimes complain, if treated according to their literal demands? When people ask for, they do not mean a crumb or a drop.

Upon a leaf she placed no more,
And set it down her guest before.
He look'd at her, and said, "This rice
For four fanāms will not suffice.
Speaking genteelly, it is true
I said a lime in size would do.
And thus a gentleman you treat!
Call this a bellyful of meat!"
She answer'd, "That's the quantity
You order'd, and no more you'll see."
He went to Rāman, and implored
His four fanāms might be restored.
Before the righteous judge the dame,
Obedient to his summons, came.
He said, "Did you this person tell
Some rice a lime in size you'd sell?"
"Yes," answer'd she, "as he desired."
"But have you done so?" he required.
"I have," she said, "as you shall know:
The very plate of rice I'll show.
In vain he tries to bring me grief:
Against his lies I fetch the leaf."
No sooner said, than off she flew,
And brought the' untasted dish to view.
"O ho!" said Rāman, "it is clear
No grain a lime in bulk is here.
The price restore, or feast his eyes
With rice each grain a lime in size."
Alarm'd she gave, with nought to say,
The money back, and went away.

The cash its owner found, you see,
As "fruit will fall beside its tree."

XIV.

'TWAS NO SUCH THING! HE'D HAD NO RING!

A dandy to a wedding went,
Sporting a ring that one had lent.
So proud the jewel to display,
He wore it after, day by day,
Until its owner saw it shine,
And said, "Return that ring of mine."
"Your ring! how can you breathe the lie?
'Tis mine: be off!" was the reply.
  The lender, full of fear and grief,
Of Mariyāthay sought relief.
Each claim'd the ring as his on oath;
And without witnesses were both.
A goldsmith should the truth decide,
Who had no interest either side.
  The trusty man was quickly brought,
Whom first in whispers Rāman taught:—
"A golden ring to you they'll show:
The touch-stone let it roughly know;
And then its quality and weight
Emphatically underrate."
  His lordship soon, handing the gold,
An officer his duty told:—
"With plaintiff and defendant go;
This jewel to yon goldsmith show,—

That he the value may declare,
And each obtain an equal share."
  When he the test severe applied,
"Gently!" the troubled owner cried.
When he asserted 'twas impure,
"Not so," said he, "you're wrong, I'm sure."
Its worth pronounced, "My property
Unjustly you appraise," cried he.
The lender's speech the assembly heard:
The borrower did not say a word.
The judge himself at once express'd
In favour of the man distress'd.
  Again the honest had his own.
This saying in the cheat was shown,—
"Who handles gold by means not fair,
To see it tested feels no care."

XV.

The mouth did hide,
And then denied.

Before they will their guilt reveal,
There are who swallow what they steal.
A woman sinn'd this double sin,
Whose next-door neighbour's fowl stepp'd in.
Its owner saw the visit paid,
But did not see an exit made.
"My fowl," she was compell'd to say,
"Enter'd your house: which is it, pray?"
"If so," the woman made reply,
"It has escaped my watchful eye."

The owner told the judge her grief,
Who question'd soon the summon'd thief.
She swore the hen she never saw;
And as no witness help'd the law,
The knowing judge, with puzzled face,
Pretended to dismiss the case.
But when they'd gone a little way,
The startled woman heard him say,—
What he intended her to hear,
Address'd to people standing near,—
"She cooks the bird she dared to steal,
And, having made her guilty meal,
Is not afraid, you see, to wear
Some of its feathers in her hair;
And impudence enough has left
Before us to deny the theft."
Raising her hand, with sudden care,
She gently felt her knot of hair.
The judge the conscious movement saw,
And call'd her back to aid the law,
Herself to witness to her shame,
With her own mouth her guilt proclaim,
And, with an added fine, to pay
A fowl for that she took away.
She proved the ancient saying sooth,—
"Shall falsehood fight and conquer truth?"

XVI.

The peas reveal'd
What they conceal'd.

About to go on pilgrimage,
What cares the Brahman's thoughts engage !
His money, by alms-begging got,
He places in a metal pot,
And to the brim, his mind to ease,
Fills it with closely shaken peas.
Then to a dear and trusty friend
He and his wife their footsteps bend,
And say, " Deposit, if you please,
Till we return, this jar of peas
In a safe place, there to remain ;
And mind you never touch a grain."
The smiling merchant gave consent ;
And on their pilgrimage they went.
It happen'd on a certain day,
When they had been some time away,
An evening party to supply
Of many guests already nigh,
No peas could anywhere be got
Save those within the Brahman's pot.
Then to his wife the trader spake,
" The peas the Brahman left we'll take,
And afterwards, when we can buy,
With other peas their place supply."
She brought the jar, the peas outpour'd ;
And then they saw the pilgrim's hoard.

The peas that had been up were down ;
The thousand pagods form'd the crown,
Till man and wife, with high delight,
Agreed to put them out of sight.
Next day more peas they chanced to' obtain,
And fill'd the rifled jar again.
  The pious pair, when months were pass'd,
From pilgrimage return'd at last ;
Took home without a thought of theft,
The jar that look'd just as 'twas left ;
Made haste its contents to outpour,
And count again their golden store ;
With changing face the peas search'd through,
And not a pagod came to view.
  The priest, exceedingly distress'd,
Regained the merchant's house ; express'd
How very much obliged he was
To him and to his wife, because
They'd kindly done as they were task'd ;
And for the cash politely ask'd.
"You nothing placed with us beside
The pot of peas," they quick replied.
  Before the judge, to end the feud,
The merchant and his wife were sued.
But Rāman could no light obtain ;
His questioning was all in vain.
He might as soon the matter clear
As give an idol ears to hear.
He had a hollow image cut,
And a detective in it shut.

The merchant and his lady both
Must take the image, and their oath,
And bear the god the temple round,
If innocent they would be found.
They wash'd their heads, and so they swore,
And then their weight of conscience bore.
When they had carried it half way,
The husband was constrain'd to say,
"What have we done? what will it cost?
To perjured persons hope is lost."
The thief was out; the spy within
Caught this confession of their sin,
And when released told every word
That in the idol's ears he'd heard.
The angry judge in threats was strong,
And made the couple own the wrong.
The thousand pagods they return'd,
And had the punishment they'd earn'd.
They found the proverb true indeed,
"God things inscrutable can read."

XVII.

One sells his rice
At any price.

A paddy*-buyer, purse in hand,
Comes to a store, and to a stand.
"I want to buy some rice," says he,
"A sample of it let me see."

* Rice in the husk.

The paddy-seller is not slow
A little measure-ful to show.
The buyer asks, " Have you no more ? "
The seller says, " This is the store :
Pagodas one or ten will buy
No other rice than now you spy."
The neighbour pays pagodas ten,
And says he'll soon be here again.
 And back he comes, with bullock strong,
To fetch his purchase before long,
And, like a man of means and mirth,
Demands his ten pagodas' worth.
The dealer brings the measure small,
And says, " Pour out, and take it all."
" This all for ten pagodas ! " cries
The purchaser. The cheat replies,
" For one or ten, I said before,
This is the rice, and there's no more.
Agreeing, ten you chose to pay,
So take your bargain, and away."
 The jest no joke the good man feels,
And to the judge the trick reveals,
To whom the storekeeper is bold
To say he's done as he was told.
Rāman ordains, " A month must glide,
Ere I this matter can decide.
Be it till then your equal doom
Your meals to eat in the same room.
You, plaintiff, the boil'd grain receive,
And just a half to this man give."

Then privately he shows his plan :
" You take a bellyful, my man ;
And break a grain of rice in two,
And give him half of it to chew."
Two meals of half a grain suffice
The hungry seller of the rice
So far that loudly he complains,
And access to the judge obtains.
Rāman the other calls, and, " Why,"
He asks, " your mess-mate's food deny ? "
Says he, " I duly dealt the meat,
One half the grain : he would not eat."
The storekeeper begins to' explain,—
" He pinches off just half one grain,
And tells me all my dinner's there :
How can I live upon such fare ? "
The buyer, " Tit for tat," replies ;
" He in a basket show'd some rice ;
' Whatever price you pay,' said he,
' This is the article you see ;'
I ten pagodas paid ; behold,
'T was but the sample that he sold !
So I the letter keep, and deal
With him by contract at each meal."
The judge now to the culprit turns,
Who with long face his sentence learns.
" According to the country-price,
His ten pagodas' worth of rice
Supply to him, or be agreed
A month on his half-rice to feed."